PREVENTION'S

LOSE WEIGHT

GUIDEBOOK

1996

BEST NEW
WEIGHT-LOSS
SECRETS
FROM
AMERICA'S TOP
DIET DOCS

EDITED BY MARK BRICKLIN
AND GALE MALESKEY OF *PREVENTION* MAGAZINE

Rodale Press, Inc.
Emmaus, Pennsylvania

Notice

This book is intended as a reference volume only, not as a medical manual. The information given here is designed to help you make informed decisions about your health. It is not intended as a substitute for any treatment that may have been prescribed by your doctor. If you suspect that you have a medical problem, we urge you to seek competent medical help.

ISBN 0–87596–304–8 hardcover

Distributed in the book trade by St. Martin's Press

2   4   6   8   10   9   7   5   3   1   hardcover

————— OUR MISSION —————

We publish books that empower people's lives.

——— RODALE 🌱 BOOKS ———

Prevention's Lose Weight Guidebook 1996 Editorial Staff

Contributors:

Rona Berg; Nick Bosco; Jonathan Bowden; Jan Bresnick; Mark Golin; William Grimes; Greg Gutfeld; Jessica B. Harris; Jayne Hurley; Corby Kummer; Bonnie Liebman; Holly McCord, R.D.; Michele Meyer; Nancy Monson; Marty Munson; Mary Nagle; Judith Olney; Cathy Perlmutter; Cheryl Sacra; Sarah Bowen Shea; Carl Sherman; Porter Shimer; Elizabeth Somer, R.D.; Maggie Spilner; Bryant Stamford, Ph.D.; Kate Staples; Holland Sweet; Rob Sweetgall

Managing Editor: Sharon Faelten
Editor: Gale Maleskey
Editor, *Prevention* Magazine: Mark Bricklin
Executive Editor, *Prevention* Magazine: Emrika Padus
Cover and Book Designers: Lisa Nawaz, Lynn N. Gano
Studio Manager: Joe Golden
Supervising Technical Artist: Kristen Morgan Downey
Technical Artist: Bernie Siegle
Permissions: Anita Small
Senior Copy Editor: Susan G. Berg
Production Manager: Helen Clogston
Manufacturing Coordinator: Melinda B. Rizzo
Office Personnel: Roberta Mulliner, Julie Kehs, Bernadette Sauerwine, Mary Lou Stephen

Rodale Health and Fitness Books

Vice-President and Editorial Director: Debora T. Yost
Art Director: Jane Colby Knutila
Research Manager: Ann Gossy Yermish
Copy Manager: Lisa D. Andruscavage

Contents

Headlines aside, most people aren't getting fatter. Here's what they're doing to stay trim while the rest of America buys relaxed-fit jeans.

I. Learn from the Experts

Think potbellies and widening bottoms are inevitable after 40? Well, weight-loss experts say you're wrong. And they tell you how to re-gain control of your weight in the middle years.

Strategically planning each day—and learning from your mistakes—can help you break through your personal weight-loss barriers and drop pounds.

"To each his own" works when it comes to weight loss—mainte-nance, too. Here are the personal tricks of people in the trade.

Use our figures to find your perfect weight, based on body mass index. Then firm up and trim down by following the experiences of more than 10,000 *Prevention* readers.

Burn fat while you sleep! Think that's a lot of baloney? Well, it's not. Your body's metabolic rate makes the difference. These three easy-to-follow tips will help keep your body's calorie-burning furnace at its hottest.

II. Make It a Habit—For Life

Even if you're not splitting wood, plowing the lower 40 or hanging laundry, you can find ways to add muscle-building, calorie-burning action to the most sedentary lifestyle. So toss out the remote control and get moving! Here's how.

Ever wonder whether the busy professionals who tell us how to stay healthy practice what they preach? From those who do, here's how.

For many people, the key to successful weight loss is a consistent walking program. Here, walking expert Rob Sweetgall explains how to make yours a habit, rain or shine.

III. Your Key to Smart Shopping

The best way to drop pounds? Cut back on calories from fat. The new food labels can help you pick low-fat foods, but there's still lots of fat hidden in all sorts of foods. Take this quiz to figure out your best low-fat selections.

IV. What You Need to Know about Nutrition

V. Turning the Tide on Temptation

Cravings aren't just psychological. They have strong physiological
components that can make some foods practically addictive. Here's
how to pick food choices that satisfy cravings without piling on
pounds.

Can you bypass bingeing by letting yourself have the treats you
crave? A new no-denial theory says yes and shows you how to still
stay in control.

These seven strategies will help you beguile your taste buds into loving low-fat foods. Honest.

VI. The Fast Track to Fitness

The perfectly executed tummy crunch, along with sensible grazing
and a few soothing mantras, will have that gut deflated in no time.
Here's how.

Getting stale? Give your exercise routine a fun change of pace—and
put some bounce in your step—with these cross-training moves.

Sore knees? Aching back? Tired feet? You can take a load off and get
a workout with soothing water exercises.

The path of most resistance—weight training—can build muscle and
reduce belly fat at any age.

Whether you're a spurter or the long, leisurely type, you can peel pounds by marking miles.

VII. Tame Down the Tension

Arm yourself with these tension-taming tactics to avoid stress-induced food binges.

High in the California redwoods, find the peace and the pace that lets you effortlessly drop pounds.

Stop overeating and other stress-related problems before they start with this energy-saving schedule.

VIII. Manage Your Emotions— And Your Weight

Most people eat to satisfy their psyches as well as their stomachs. Here's how to manage your emotions—and your weight.

A language-induced attitude adjustment can steer your thoughts away from food and toward a slim, new future.

Is a poor body image keeping you from being trim and slim? Here's how to get out and get moving even when your body isn't perfect.

There's a new breed of therapist who will help you confront your self-image problems—and do something about them.

IX. Low-Fat, No-Fuss Feasts

Introduction

Headlines aside, most people aren't getting fatter. Here's what they're doing to stay trim while the rest of America buys relaxed-fit jeans.

"Americans: Fatter Than Ever." That headline glared at us from newspapers across the country last year. The text told the unsettling tale. The country's biggest long-term nutrition survey, the National Health and Nutrition Examination Survey (NHANES III for short), found that in just a few short years, the number of people who qualify as obese had risen from one in four to one in three. That meant that 58 million people in America tipped the scales at more than 20 percent of their ideal weights. "If this were about tuberculosis, it would be called an epidemic," proclaimed one public health official.

In the aftermath of all of this bad news, researchers came up with some good news. In speculating about what went wrong for the people who had gained weight, they also inadvertently confirmed what the two-thirds majority of Americans are doing right to keep their weights normal.

In the simplest terms, of course, overweight Americans got that way because they consumed more calories than they burned as energy. The NHANES III survey found that on average, people are eating 100 to 300 calories more a day now than they were a decade or so ago. That may not sound like much, but it adds up, on average, to an extra eight pounds per person.

How are people getting those additional calories? Well, they're not eating more fat, apparently, since fat consumption has dropped slightly, from about 38 to 35 percent of calories. (That's still higher than many doctors think healthy, though.)

Experts speculate that as people turn away from high-fat foods, they're inadvertently gravitating toward sugar, assuming any low-fat food can be consumed in massive quantities.

Eating as much as you want may work just fine when it's broccoli or brown rice or apples. After all, few people eat more than two or three servings of that stuff. But it doesn't apply to many of the admittedly tasty low-fat snacks developed to appeal to the fat-conscious consumer. That's because these foods are loaded with sugar and have just as many calories as the high-fat versions.

Yet no one is ready to do without these dandy new foods. And that's where we come in. We detail how the two-thirds majority—the two in three people who succeed in losing weight and keeping it off—use low-fat salad dressings, cheeses, dairy products and spreads in ways that offer substantial savings in calories. At the same time, we tip you off on surprising sources of hidden sugar: salad dressings, frozen dinners and bran cereals, among others.

We show you how to make the most of the new, easier-to-read food labels. Serving size and calories do count! (Find out how sugar can be disguised by many different names.)

And we provide you with recipes for good-tasting dishes that replace fat with fiber and the nutrients you need.

It's no surprise that those in our two-thirds majority also are more likely to be breaking a sweat than their portly counterparts. Whether they are intentionally exercising or simply walking the dog, taking the stairs or pruning a rosebush, they're active. And that makes all the difference.

Weight-loss experts agree: Permanent weight loss is doomed without exercise. That's because your metabolism actually slows as you eat less, so you burn fewer of the calories you consume.

So we show you how to get around that by revving up your metabolism with exercise, even if you've never exercised before in your life and no matter what your age. We show you how to whittle your waistline, beef up your biceps and tone your thighs in as little as 20 minutes a day.

We even tell you what weight-loss experts do to stay slim. Sure, they have their moments of temptation, just like everyone. But they've discovered what works for them, whether it's keeping a pair of walking shoes handy, wearing waist-cinching clothes for social occasions to avoid overeating or commuting by bicycle. As you'll see, everyone is different. The trick is finding what works for you. And we provide plenty of practical alternatives.

In fact, if you're one of the overweight minority, here's one tip you can use right now: If you walk briskly for just 30 minutes, four times a week, you'll burn about 600 calories a week. That adds up to almost nine pounds over the course of a year. Keep at it, and you'll never need to diet again.

Did we mention that we included an entire section on how to make good health a habit for life?

—*The Editors*

Part I
Learn from the Experts

Reverse Middle-Age Spread

Think potbellies and widening bottoms are inevitable after 40? Well, weight-loss experts say you're wrong. And they tell you how to regain control of your weight in the middle years.

If there's one thing that's inevitable after age 40, it's middle-age spread. Or is it? Is accumulation of extra pounds after 40 really written in our genes, our hormones and the laws of nature?

It's a fact that on average, men and women do tend to put on weight as they get older, until about age 55, when weight starts to decrease. And many women fear that the hormonal reshuffling called menopause will guarantee a new deal of flab. It's true: As a woman reaches menopause, her hourglass figure may start looking more like a crystal ball as excess fat accumulates around her middle. And in the middle years, men may begin to see the rise of the infamous potbelly. These changes, of course, raise the risk of heart disease, stroke, high blood pressure, diabetes and cancer.

But the fact is, nowhere is it written that middle-age spread must surely befall you. Research suggests that though the phenomenon is widespread, it's not inevitable—not even in menopause. Experts say that contrary to the common notion, hormones probably are not entirely to blame for the thickening middles of middle age.

"Whenever we've done studies where women take estrogen or a placebo, both groups have gained equal amounts of weight," says Brian Walsh, M.D., director of the menopause clinic at Brigham and Women's Hospital in Boston. More likely, the weight gain of middle age is caused by the slowdown in metabolism that accompanies aging in both women and men. And much of this slowdown has to do with lowered activity levels.

> **A** SEDENTARY LIFESTYLE EXPLAINS **70** PERCENT OF THE DIFFERENCE IN WEIGHT GAIN BETWEEN OLDER AND YOUNGER PEOPLE.

"A sedentary lifestyle explains 70 percent of the difference in weight gain between older and younger people," says William J. Evans, Ph.D., director of the Noll Physiological Research Center at Pennsylvania State University in University Park.

"The problem starts from the mid-twenties on," concurs James M. Rippe, M.D., director of the Center for Clinical and Lifestyle Research, affiliated with Tufts University School of Medicine in Boston. "People become imperceptibly less active as their lives become busier."

The evolution from hot tomato to couch potato usually coincides with the onset of adult responsibilities at around age 25. Grown-ups no longer have the time, the desire or the ability to stay out dancing all night after a full workday. All too often the couch beckons us once the dishes have been cleared off the dinner table. Or the baby needs bathing, and the kids need us to help them with their homework.

This kickback in physical activity costs us, says Dr. Rippe.

"Inactive people lose a half-pound of muscle a year—that's five pounds a decade of the body's most metabolically active tissue," he says. "Yet most people continue to eat the way they did when they were younger. So in many ways, middle-age weight gain is really no different from the way you gained weight when you were younger. It's still due to taking in more calories than you expend in physical activity." The difference, then, has more to do with where we store excess fat.

> **I**NACTIVE PEOPLE LOSE
> **A HALF-POUND OF MUSCLE**
> **A YEAR—**
> **FIVE POUNDS A DECADE.**

Fat around the Middle

Sex hormones may not make you add pounds but may determine where you put them. "Both sexes have estrogens and androgens, but the former predominate in women, and the latter, in men," says Dr. Walsh. These hormones may account for some of the difference in fat distribution between the sexes, although heredity largely accounts for the rest. Many women are pear-shaped, holding weight around the hips and thighs. "Stomach fat is a marker for androgens," says Dr. Walsh. "As a woman's estrogen level declines with age, the proportion of androgens rises. Women with high androgen levels tend to become apple-shaped, gaining weight around the middle, the way men do."

Fat around your middle is also considered a marker for disease. In fact, the effects of your body shape on your health can be roughly quantified using the waist-to-hip ratio (WHR). Simply measure your waist at its narrowest point, measure your hips at their widest point, then divide your waist measurement by your hip measurement.

Debbie Gardiner: No More Big Sweaters

She stands five feet four inches, but Debbie Gardiner never really looked petite until recently.

At one time, the 43-year-old New York City advertising manager weighed in at 140 pounds and favored big sweaters to disguise a thick middle and chunky hips. Today, she is 35 pounds and three dress sizes smaller. She now tucks in her tops and looks younger than she did ten years ago.

Debbie made a two-pronged attack on her widening waist. She committed to walking for an hour each day and cutting way back on the fat in her diet. She had never exercised on a regular basis, but she always had to do a lot of walking around the city because of her job. She decided that the best way to fit in a walking program would be to wake up a couple of hours earlier each morning, since she had the most energy then.

"Now I walk between four and five miles every morning and about seven or eight on weekends," she says. The weekday walks take about an hour; the weekend walks, about two. Debbie doesn't miss a day, rain or shine, unless the weather gets really treacherous.

Simple changes in Debbie's diet also helped peel off the pounds. "I used to eat a typical American diet, including pizza and hamburgers. But I've really cut back on fat. I took all of my favorite foods and figured out ways to lower their fat content. And once I started that and the walking, the weight just came off." After a few months, the fat cravings seemed to disappear. Not that she won't eat an occasional hamburger or a dessert. "My feeling is that if you really want something, just have it, or you'll eat your way around it."

Men whose WHRs exceed 0.9 are more prone to heart disease, high blood pressure, stroke, diabetes and certain forms of cancer. Women whose WHRs exceed 0.8 are also at risk for these ills. The WHR is such a strong predictor that it is now considered an independent risk factor for diabetes, heart disease and even peptic ulcers. That means that even if you are not obese (20 percent above your ideal weight, according to the Metropolitan Life Insurance Company tables), you are still at high risk for chronic disease if your WHR is too high. If you are obese and have a high WHR, you are doubly at risk.

40-Plus Workouts

Fortunately, middle-age spread is no more difficult to slim than any other weight gain. Exercise is key. And though exercise alone (without weight loss) has a relatively small effect on your risk for chronic disease, a modest weight loss of, say, five to ten pounds could have a major, positive impact on your health.

Research seems to suggest two effective approaches to exercising for weight loss: (1) long-term raising of your metabolism to burn more calories and (2) "spot burning" of excess fat and calories. The ideal weight-loss program would combine these two approaches.

Dr. Evans's research indicates that muscle-making resistance training (the first method) may be the single most effective weapon you can employ against over-40 weight gain. That's because aerobic activities such as walking, running and swimming (the second method) burn calories for only as long as you are doing them. But weight training can help increase your metabolism over the long haul by building metabolically active muscle. That means you continue burning calories even after you stop exercising for the day.

If you are already physically active, lifting weights at

least two or three times a week to work your major muscle groups should pay off in trimming inches and raising your metabolic rate. Dr. Rippe points out that women should emphasize working out the muscles in the lower body, since these are the largest weight-bearing muscles and so will burn the most calories.

For people over age 40 who have become less and less active over the years, Dr. Rippe recommends starting easy. He urges people to up their everyday activity in small ways. Stop using the remote control and extension phones. Park your car a few blocks from the office and walk. Take the stairs instead of the elevator. He also advocates working up to walking at least four times a week.

You needn't walk at a heart-thumping pace to get results. According to a study at the Cooper Aerobics Center in Dallas, the most effective fat-burning workout may be slow, sustained walking. While carbohydrates are the body's fuel of choice for high-intensity exercise, theorizes John Duncan, Ph.D., chief of clinical applications at the center, fat is the best fuel for sustained low-intensity exercise. The fat-burning effect kicks in after 20 minutes. So Dr. Duncan says that you should begin with a walk at an easy pace—say, 20 minutes a mile—for more than 20 minutes, working up to an hour.

40-Plus Eating

As important as exercise is, no weight-control plan is complete unless it addresses what you eat and how much. Since the over-40 metabolism has slowed from reduced activity and the muscle loss that accompanies it, people have to step up their vigilance over fat and calories.

Many experts agree that for most people over age 40, the easiest and most effective way to achieve this goal is to

(continued on page 10)

Susan Flagg: A New Swimsuit Figure

By the time Susan Flagg turned 40, she had to buy a whole new wardrobe in a larger size. At five feet three inches, she wasn't plump—in fact, she weighed only 118. But the pounds had piled on gradually during her thirties, when she took her first sedentary job as a magazine editor and then gave birth to her son a few years later.

Susan had managed to stay fit by swimming, walking, taking low-impact aerobics classes and eating in a nutrition-conscious way. But none of this was enough to keep the pounds at bay.

"I was disappointed when I read that swimming, my favorite exercise, wasn't great for weight loss," she says. "And I was always a hearty eater, so I wasn't happy when I realized that I couldn't eat like I always had. I was used to listening to my appetite, so I felt like it was betraying me. I figured I'd have to just kiss my youthful metabolism good-bye."

A few years ago, an executive at her company recruited some employees for an eight-week program to study the effects of weight training on body fat, weight and blood pressure. The recruits had to have done no resistance training for at least five years, if ever.

"We were encouraged to work out together as a class for 45 minutes, three times a week," says Susan. "We began lifting very light weights at first, using Nautilus and Cybex equipment and some free weights, focusing on proper form. The repetitions were 8 to 12 for the upper body and 12 to 15 for the lower body. We increased our weights gradually with the supervision of our trainer. And since we all worked out together, we weren't intimidated by the muscular men using the equipment.

"To my surprise, I took to weight training from the start. I am a solitary exerciser by nature, so I loved setting my own pace and watching my strength increase while my pounds decreased. During those eight weeks, the pounds came off slowly but steadily. I lost four pounds, and my body fat started dropping, too, from 24.8 percent when I started to 23 percent at the end of the eight weeks. So many of us loved the class that we asked the program director if we could extend the class another eight weeks. I enjoyed my routines so much that even on vacation I took along free weights and stretch bands."

Susan continued to swim twice a week, though after the first year she had to stop for a while because of scheduling and sinus problems. She substituted an hour of vigorous walking twice a week. And she didn't stop weight training when the program ended. In fact, she started asking for help using more of the free weights. By the end of her first year, she had dropped 14 pounds. "Not only had I lost weight, but my shape had changed as well. My waist and hips got smaller, my tummy got flatter, and I added nice shape to my legs. I went down two sizes in my skirts and slacks but stayed the same size on top by building up my shoulders, chest and back. None of my clothes fit anymore.

"I guess I hadn't caught up with my new muscles' need for more fuel. I made an effort to eat more and continued to increase the weights I was using, because the challenge was fun."

At the end of her second year of weight training, Susan had gained back about four pounds—and it was all muscle. Now in her midforties, she weighs 108. When her body fat was measured, she found that she's down to 15 percent, just like a professional athlete.

"Not only am I firm all over, but I look forward to trying on swimsuits. I've also discovered that resistance training reduces stress and gives me an afterglow, as swimming does. I'm also hungrier than I used to be, but now I can trust my appetite to guide me again."

eat a low-fat diet loaded with fruits, vegetables, whole grains, legumes and other complex carbohydrates.

This approach has several advantages. First, by going for such low-fat fare, you trim down the source of calories that's primary in most people's diets. (Fat contains far more calories than either protein or carbohydrates.) Second, you cut your chances of adding body fat to your frame, because dietary fat is more readily converted into body fat than protein or carbohydrates. Third, because complex carbohydrates are comparatively low in calories (they're not as calorie-dense as fat or protein), you can virtually eat as much of them as you want and not feel deprived.

> **O**VERWEIGHT PEOPLE UNDERESTIMATE THEIR DAILY CALORIC INTAKES BY **40** PERCENT EACH DAY, AND LEAN PEOPLE, BY **20** PERCENT.

One study suggests that those who use this low-fat, high-carb method of weight control are generally more satisfied than those who try dietary restriction (simple calorie cutting). People trying the low-fat approach reported that their meals were more palatable and more filling than the calorie cutters reported.

If you stick to such low-fat foods, you can let your appetite tell you when it's time to stop eating. But if you stray from this fare, you might have to invoke portion control and limit the amount you eat.

In studies cited by Thomas A. Wadden, Ph.D., director of the weight and eating disorders program at the University of Pennsylvania in Philadelphia, both overweight and lean people tended to underestimate their daily calorie counts. One study found that overweight people underestimated their intakes by 40 percent each day, and lean people, by 20 percent.

Dr. Wadden teaches portion control and urges people to be especially careful when they are choosing processed foods, which can be high in fat or low in fat but high in calories. Also, with processed foods, even some low-fat meals contain high amounts of sodium and sugar and are low in fiber. He urges his patients to limit their daily fat intakes to 25 percent of calories.

Probably the most enthusiastic advocate of the low-fat, high-carb approach is Dean Ornish, M.D., author of *Eat More, Weigh Less*. Dr. Ornish, who is also director of the Preventive Medicine Research Institute in Sausalito, California, advocates a radical reduction in fat to less than 10 percent of your total daily calories. You can do this without relying on a calculator by following a vegetarian diet that emphasizes the fiber-filled foods—fruits, vegetables and grains. According to Dr. Ornish, you must also substitute beans and legumes for meats, restrict dairy products to nonfat or very low fat and avoid oils, sugars, alcohol and fatty foods (such as avocados, olives, nuts and seeds) as well as any processed food with more than two grams of fat per serving. This can help you feel full and enable you to eat a lot of nutrition-packed foods while you lose weight.

This second approach may sound tougher to follow than it actually is. According to Dr. Ornish, "When you restrict calories, the body perceives this as starvation and slows the metabolism so that it burns those calories more slowly. When you change the type of food you eat, you don't have to reduce the amount of food, so your metabolism doesn't slow down—it may actually increase. Also, it costs calories to convert carbohydrates and protein to fat.

"So if you shift from a diet of 40 percent fat to one of 10 percent fat, you'll get one-third fewer calories for the same amount of food, and it will be harder for the body to store these calories as body fat. You'll feel not only less deprived but also more energetic. And you'll be protecting yourself against the diseases that are linked with the typical American diet, such as heart disease, high blood pressure, breast and prostate cancer, diabetes and osteoporosis."

If the under–10 percent plan sounds unmanageable or you do not want to go strictly vegetarian, Dr. Ornish urges you to stick to one occasional small portion of roasted or grilled skinless chicken breast or lean fish, such as perch, sole, cod or flounder, and clams, mussels, scallops and oysters. Whatever your choice, your fat should not exceed 25 percent of your daily calories.

—Jan Bresnick with Gloria McVeigh and Linda Rao

Lots of Little Ways to Lose a Lot of Weight

Strategically planning each day—and learning from your mistakes—can help you break through your personal weight-loss barriers and drop pounds.

Millions of Americans face the weight-loss front today. Some people are just thinking about battling their bulging bellies. Others have lost a few—or maybe many—pounds but need to do more to reach their goals. It isn't that people don't know the basic math: Eat fewer calories, exercise more. It's that they don't know how to make that equation work in their day-to-day lives.

Weight loss isn't attained by only one decision. It's the culmination of thousands of decisions made day in and day out. And there are lots of ways to make those decisions easier, less complicated, even enjoyable. We asked some of the country's leading experts in nutrition, physiology and psychology for their best tips on how to help you, whether you're trying to lose your first pound or your 50th.

Plan, Plan, Plan

You've probably heard the old saying "Failing to plan is planning to fail." And many of our weight-loss experts agree that planning, in a variety of forms, is what makes the difference between a successful weight-loss strategy and one that never gets legs.

If you set goals and don't make plans to meet them, you'll fall back into the same eating and exercise patterns you're used to. Many of the suggestions we got from the experts are about taking the time to set goals and plan each and every day for the ways you'll meet them.

> **A**FTER AN INDULGENCE, DON'T BLAME YOURSELF FOR LACK OF WILLPOWER. JUST EVALUATE HOW YOU CAN PLAN BETTER TO AVOID IT IN THE FUTURE.

Keep a food diary. Choose a way to keep track of what and when you eat every day. You may choose to track fat grams, calories, exchanges— the method is up to you. It seems that just keeping track is what helps people cut back, not brutal honesty or a foolproof memory. In fact, when starting out, don't even try to make any changes. Just get an idea of what it is you're eating every day to maintain the weight that you are.

Crush mall cravings. If you're going to the mall and you know you're going to smell pizza or cinnamon buns that will make your mouth water, be prepared. Eat before you go out, so you won't be as temptable. And don't shop until you drop. Plan a snack that fits into your calorie/fat gram plan. Either carry it with you or know just where to purchase it.

Learn the ten-minute rule. If a craving for a hot fudge sundae hits and it's not in your plan for the day, distract yourself for at least ten minutes. In most cases, the craving will pass. Meditate, call a friend, go for a walk. If after ten minutes your craving hasn't subsided, you may truly be hungry. Look for a healthy low-fat snack.

Plan to eat at home. That's one of the few places

where you really know what you're putting in your mouth. But if your lifestyle demands eating out or occasional fast fixes, plan for them. Most fast-food eateries supply handy pamphlets describing in detail the caloric and fat content of their menu items. Collect these pamphlets and analyze them for your favorite low-fat meals. Then when you have to make a stop, you know just what to order without even looking at the choices.

For more expensive restaurants, call ahead and ask what's low-fat and low-calorie on the menu. Many places will prepare special meals if you give them notice. Poring over the menu when you get there puts too many tempting images in your mind.

Don't plan on willpower. Physiology always beats out psychology. In other words, hunger beats out self-control. To get around that, try to plan your day so that you aren't forced to use self-control. It's the old "Don't go grocery shopping on an empty stomach" idea. Expand that concept to your whole day. After an indulgence, don't blame yourself for lack of willpower. Just evaluate how you can plan better to avoid it in the future.

Get a New Attitude

Changing your lifestyle means changing your attitude toward a lot of things. You set new priorities, and you learn new likes and dislikes. Be ready to incorporate new ideas to help you change old habits.

Set goals and priorities. Spend some time working out your goals on paper. It's important that they're not vague. It's also important that they're reasonable. If you're not sure if your weight-loss goals are reasonable, seek out a qualified health professional to give you an objective perspective.

Take stock of your shelves. Look through your pantry

and your refrigerator, and get rid of any foods that don't fit in with your new goals for weight control. Donate them to a local charity and then restock with foods that fit in with your new meal plans. There are lots of new foods on the market that can help you cut calories and fat without sacrificing taste.

GIVE YOUR DORITOS TO CHARITY.

You can change just about any favorite high-fat meal into a low-fat version.

Read about it. Read a lot about weight loss, diet, nutrition and exercise. You not only may find it motivating and inspiring, but you also should have more ideas to help you tailor a program that meets your needs. One study has shown that people who take the bull by the horns and design their own programs are the most successful at losing weight and keeping it off.

Focus on maintenance. There is a possibility that weight cycling (losing, gaining, losing) is linked with bad health. A fear of weight cycling, however, should not deter anyone from attempting to reach a healthy weight. Lately, a popular theory has been that most people who lose weight eventually gain it back (and then some)—which may fast become a self-fulfilling prophecy. The problem is, most studies on people losing weight are done in clinical or hospital settings. And often those people comply with special weight reduction programs as long as they are active (or captive) participants. When they go home, they go back to old habits. People who design their own programs at home often are much more successful at maintaining their weight losses. Just look around you. Chances are you know people who've lost weight and kept it off for years. And you thought they were exceptions to the rule!

Know serving sizes. Counting fat grams is not enough.

Studies show that people can still gain weight when eating a low-fat diet. They may load up on low-fat foods. It's important to watch the total amount of food you eat. Portion control is essential. The American Heart Association puts out a pamphlet called *The American Heart Association Diet*, which gives tips on determining portions. Call 1-800-242-8721 to order the brochure. Spend some time measuring out portions and seeing what they look like on the plate, so you can judge when to stop serving yourself. Do you really know what a cup of spaghetti looks like?

Use the one-to-one rule. Use fat-free and sugar-free products, but use them wisely. A one-to-one substitution is best. In other words, substitute one fat-free Twinkie for one regular Twinkie. Don't kid yourself into thinking you can eat two or three because they're low in fat. Sugary calories add up to fat in your body.

> **D**O YOU REALLY KNOW WHAT A CUP OF SPAGHETTI LOOKS LIKE?

Make room for goodies. Don't feel you have to ban chocolate or any other favorite food. If you watch your portions and/or your calories, you can find room for any food. Depriving yourself may set you up for bingeing.

Exercise Smart

To lose weight and keep it off, exercise has to become a regular part of your everyday life—no ifs, ands or "but I don't have the time" about it. If you don't have time for exercise, you don't have the means for permanent weight control. Once you realize it's the only way out, you may begin to find the time you need.

Team up with your doctor. In a survey by the President's Council on Physical Fitness and Sports, respondents said they thought they would be more motivated to exercise if their doctors told them to. If you feel like you fall into that category, find a doctor who will encourage you. Although there are no studies to confirm the results for weight loss, studies have shown that doctors' encouragement definitely helps people quit smoking.

Learn to love resistance training. Maintaining or increasing your lean body mass is a crucial component of the weight-loss game plan. The more muscle you have, the more calories you burn, whether you're exercising or sleeping. Weight lifting is a unique exercise in that it enhances lean body mass. While aerobic activities such as walking, jogging and bicycling are important for fat burning, they don't substantially increase lean body mass. And as we age, that lean body mass tends to decrease.

Weight training should be done two or three times a week, unless you target different muscle groups on different days, in which case you can work out more often.

Learn the 80 percent solution. To increase muscle mass, you need to do high-intensity weight training. That means finding the weight that you can lift about 8 to 12 times and no more. At that rate, you're lifting about 80 percent of your capacity. (If you lift a weight 25 times without tiring, you tone your muscles, but you don't increase muscle mass.) It's fine to start with lighter weights to train your muscles to get ready for heavier work.

EXPERTS SAY MAKING TIME FOR EXERCISE IS WHAT SPELLS "SUCCESS."

Walk and weight train. To lose weight, most people need to commit to at least 45 to 60 minutes of low-intensity endurance training, such as brisk walking, almost every day. So if you're lifting weights one day, you should still try to get your walk in. (We know it's hard.) Unless you are a bodybuilder and need to maximize your output in one area, you can do both and enhance your weight-loss program without harming your body. Try doing one in the morning and the other in the late afternoon or evening, to avoid fatigue.

Try dumbbells. You don't have to invest in an expensive home gym or in a membership in a fitness center to weight-train. To start out, buy a $20 set of barbells with instructions and work out at home. You can see how you like it without a big investment. If you're unsure how to use your barbells, seek instruction from a certified health and fitness instructor at your local YWCA or fitness club. As you progress, you may find fitness centers great places to meet lifting buddies or to learn more about your new sport.

Keep a journal. Just like food diaries, exercise journals help keep you motivated to do what it is you want to do. Keep one for weight lifting to show your progress and keep another for aerobic activity. If you're not keen on spending a full hour exercising continuously, remember that it's the total amount of exercise you do in one day that matters most, not whether you do it all at the same time. Four 15-minute sessions are as effective at burning calories as one continuous hour.

Find some good videos. Ask your friends if they have any favorite workout videos. Keep a collection around, so you can vary your workout from time to time to avoid boredom. You can even borrow videos from your local public library to keep things interesting. Instead of a walk outside, go inside and try step aerobics—or polka or country-western dancing. Just don't try to do the whole tape the first day out. Ease into it, or you may be too sore to get out of bed the next day.

Do Some Mental Exercise

Many of our barriers to weight loss are mental and emotional ones. While some people may need counseling to break through their weight-loss walls, others can use simple mental techniques to help institute healthy habits.

Visualize your goal and how you'll get there. Spend some time every day visualizing yourself at your ideal and realistic weight. See yourself doing the behaviors you need to do to obtain the results you want. Use all of your senses to imagine yourself enjoying a delicious apple if you need to eat more fruit. Or vividly imagine how you'll feel on a brisk morning walk.

De-stress to fight fat. Stress might have an impact on the way your body metabolizes fat. In addition to that, you may eat more when you're feeling pressured. So find ways to reduce the effects of stress, such as walking or meditation. Do whatever you need to do to keep your life in balance.

Stop negative self-talk. Become aware of all of the little ways you sabotage yourself through your thoughts. We all occasionally carry on internal dialogues that can stand in the way of success. Catch yourself saying "I'll never lose weight" or "I hate to exercise" and replace those thoughts with more positive ones.

Learn relapse prevention. It's normal to relapse—to go back to being a slug or eating high-fat foods—for a day, a week or even longer. That's part of the pattern of change and growth, not the end of your weight-loss efforts. When it happens, use it as a learning experience. Ask yourself what was going on in your life when the relapse occurred. Family pressures? Work stress? Your sister Mary offering you homemade chocolate cake? Then try to make plans to meet those relapse triggers more successfully in the future.

Get more sleep. Many people work too hard and get too little sleep. We may even eat to compensate for our lack of sleep. It may give us a quick boost, but we end up storing the extra calories as fat. When you need to work long hours, try walks or showers rather than candy bars to boost your energy.

—Maggie Spilner with Therese Walsh

How America's Top Diet Docs Stay Trim

"To each his own" works when it comes to weight loss—maintenance, too. Here are the personal tricks of people in the trade.

Weight-loss experts are a little like superheros, aren't they? They can leap tall restaurant dessert tables without a single, longing glance. They can drop five pounds faster than you can drop a second helping of dumplings onto your plate. They receive their magical slimming powers from a secret body of complex knowledge that only they have access to.

Not true. In fact, most weight-loss experts are just like us. They have their moments of temptation. They have challenges that must be met with confidence, proper diet and exercise. And believe it or not, many of them keep their weight down not so much by employing nutritional charts, calorie-burning equations and high-tech equipment as by using a few simple techniques on a daily basis.

After all, the key to losing 20 pounds isn't a

crash diet. You need to chip away a pound or two a week using smart, realistic strategies. We talked with some of the nation's top weight-loss doctors and asked them one simple question: What are the little things that you do in your life to manage your weight?

KEN COOPER, M.D.
Cooper Aerobics Center, Dallas

"If you want real motivation to help you continue an exercise program, get a dog," says Dr. Cooper. "I have a little dog that I walk with every day. The only problem is that I walk so fast now that she can't keep up with me, so I have to carry her in my arms—much to the amusement of my neighbors."

But the real secret of how he has maintained his weight for the past 34 years, he says, is an evening workout. "I go for a run before dinner and find that it reduces my appetite. I'm thirsty but not too hungry. Studies have shown that a surefire way to put on weight is by getting a lot of

> **IF YOU WANT REAL MOTIVATION TO HELP YOU CONTINUE AN EXERCISE PROGRAM, GET A DOG.**

calories in the evening, as opposed to spreading them more evenly through the day. So I try to eat solidly at breakfast and lunch, and then my run in the evening ensures that dinner doesn't turn into a feast."

JOHN FOREYT, PH.D.
Baylor University, Waco, Texas

Dr. Foreyt has jogged his way through *Pride and Prejudice, Moby Dick, Don Quixote de la Mancha* and many other classic novels—by listening to audiotapes while he runs. "I try to put in 52 minutes a day, seven days a week. What really gets me motivated to do it is books on tape."

Dr. Foreyt used to jog to music. "But that got kind of old. Now I'm getting in my exercise and getting a chance to 'read' all of the books I don't normally have time for. I'm not quite as dedicated about my eating and exercising when I'm on the road. But one way I try to make the situation more encouraging is to book rooms in hotels that I know are near great places to jog."

DAYLE HAYES, R.D.
Deaconess Medical Center, Billings, Montana

Whenever possible, Hayes likes to take active vacations. "River rafting, skiing—anything that gets the body moving," she says.

Hayes likes to work in physical activity on the job as well: "Rather than meeting over a cup of coffee, I like to suggest that we take a walk." And just so she's always prepared, Hayes is never far from a comfortable pair of walking shoes. "I keep them in my briefcase," she smiles. "That way, even if I'm stuck in a large airport during a layover, I can go for a hike."

> **I** take active vacations— river rafting, skiing, anything that gets the body moving.

When Hayes does have time for a serious workout, she keeps herself motivated to go the distance. "I listen to books on tape. That way, I'll want to extend my workout just to find out how the chapter ends!"

Along with her walking shoes and cassettes, Hayes is never without some kind of fruit or another low-fat food. "I take food in the car, on planes and to the office," she explains. "That way, when I'm hungry, I don't have to rely on whatever happens to be around, such as candy bars or fast food."

SUSAN ZELITCH YANOVSKI, M.D.
National Institute of Diabetes and Digestive and Kidney Diseases, Bethesda, Maryland

"One of my biggest challenges is trying to incorporate physical activity into my busy schedule," says Dr. Yanovski. "So I try to take small opportunities to get moving—even something as simple as getting up to change channels on the television instead of using the remote control."

Dr. Yanovski has found many moments during the day to put her technique into practice. "If I go to the store, I'll park in the space farthest away from the entrance and walk it. And I never use an elevator if I can find some stairs instead." Because of her busy schedule, Dr. Yanovski finds herself eating in restaurants quite a bit. "It's a big challenge to eat out and not gain weight," she admits. "One thing I always try to do is eat slower than everyone else at my table. That way, while everyone else is going back to the buffet for seconds or ordering dessert, I'm still working on my original platter."

MORTON H. SHAEVITZ, PH.D.
Institute for Family and Work Relationships, La Jolla, California

Dr. Shaevitz loves food. But he has managed to turn what may seem like a critical drawback into an advantage. "Because I do love food, I never eat a meal unless I have enough time to really sit down and enjoy it," he says. "People tend to eat poorly when rushed, grabbing the first thing at hand. Instead, I'll have a small snack such as an apple or a bagel, which will hold me over until I can eat a full meal in leisure."

Dr. Shaevitz keeps a careful eye on the factors that tend to make him lose control of his eating, such as fatigue, Chinese restaurants and bad company. "If you watch yourself closely, you quickly recognize moments when you have less control—and you can make sure to avoid those situations."

Dr. Shaevitz gives himself the occasional day off. "Once a month, I might have something like a hamburger and french fries or a few pieces of pepperoni pizza. One meal isn't really going to do any damage, and then I don't feel deprived."

> **O**NCE A MONTH, I MIGHT HAVE SOMETHING LIKE A HAMBURGER AND FRENCH FRIES OR A FEW PIECES OF PEPPERONI PIZZA.

SACHIKO T. ST. JEOR, R.D., PH.D.
University of Nevada School of Medicine, Reno

"Some people make it a point not to wear formfitting clothes when they go out to eat. This way, they won't be uncomfortable or look bad when they eat too much," says Dr. St. Jeor. "Instead, I'll often wear something formfitting, which helps remind me not to overeat."

To make sure she doesn't challenge the boundaries of the clothes she wears, Dr. St. Jeor practices a form of restrained eating. "Rather than ordering a whole dessert for myself and eating only a little bit of it, I try not to order one at all, or I'll share one with a friend," she says.

"First of all, a bite of this and a bite of that can really add up. And second, why put yourself through the temptation of ordering a dessert, having one bite and then sitting there while the rest of it stares you in the face?" Dr. St. Jeor takes her weight-loss cues directly from her weight scale. "I know what I should weigh, and I check myself about once a week, because the first few extra pounds gained may not be readily recognized."

DENISE MARECKI, R.D.
University of Michigan Clinical Research Center, Ann Arbor

Marecki allows little room for mistakes. "I try to stick to a very basic breakfast and lunch routine during the week," she says. "Breakfast is either a bowl of cereal or a bagel and fruit, and lunch is either a bowl of soup or a salad." Marecki claims that she usually runs into trouble when she allows herself more variation. "But if I can stick to that menu during the week, I will give myself more flexibility on the weekend. And this schedule seems to work."

Marecki also watches her alcohol intake. "The calories can really add up, so I usually allow myself only one or two glasses of wine on the weekend."

JAMES KENNEY, R.D., PH.D.
Pritikin Longevity Center, Santa Monica, California

Dr. Kenney says that he doesn't deny feelings of hunger and that he also doesn't pay attention to how much he eats. "But I do pay attention to what I eat," he says. "I used to be quite a chocolate chip ice cream and doughnut fiend, but I no longer give in to the temptation of high-fat foods."

For Dr. Kenney, the concept of substitution has been something of a saving grace. "Instead of a doughnut, I now have a cinnamon-raisin bagel, and instead of high-fat ice cream, I choose chocolate fat-free, sugar-free frozen yogurt. And the one heartening thing I've noticed is that giving up high-fat temptations does get easier the longer you keep at it."

JONATHAN ROBISON, PH.D.
Michigan Center for Preventive Medicine, Lansing

Dr. Robison controls his weight by not making weight control an obsession. "I believe that there's no such thing as a forbidden food," he says. "Everything is okay sometimes. The key thing for me is to eat three meals at regular times, so I'm never too hungry at any given moment."

THE MORE INTERESTING THE FOOD, THE EASIER I FIND IT IS TO SATISFY MY APPETITE.

But just because he eats at regular intervals doesn't mean the food he eats has to be regular. "I like a wide variety of colors, textures, tastes and aromas. The more interesting the food, the easier I find it is to satisfy my appetite."

Like many of us, he sometimes uses food as an emotional outlet. "But even that's okay occasionally," he says. "I know I'm doing it, I know why I need to do it, and therefore I can control it. Luckily, food is not my only emotional outlet."

RONETTE KOLOTKIN, PH.D.
Duke University, Durham, North Carolina

A date with her NordicTrack four times a week is how Dr. Kolotkin keeps her weight in check. But she also gets a little help from her husband. "I'm a sweetaholic—particularly a chocoholic," she admits. "So I have an arrangement with my husband, who eats sweets on a daily basis, to keep them hidden from me. It's an arrangement that works well."

One thing in particular can trigger Dr. Kolotkin's sweet tooth: "Stress. So instead of reaching for a candy bar, I play a tape of New Age music called *Ocean Dreams*. It is very relaxing and has a lot fewer calories!"

JAMES O. HILL, PH.D.
University of Colorado Health Sciences Center, Denver

"Exercise is how I keep my weight down. In particular, I have a preference for tennis," says Dr. Hill. "When I can, I play three or four times a week. And if I can get that in, I don't have to worry so much about what I eat."

Of course, Dr. Hill has those days when the couch seems a little more attractive than the court. "To get myself motivated, I think not about the actual exercise but rather about how good I'll feel when it's finished. That gets me going."

Who has time to spend an hour a day, several days a week, exercising? "Well, just ask yourself this," says Dr. Hill. "If you could make an extra $5,000 a week in only five hours, would you do it? You bet you would. So you do have the time . . . it's just a matter of seeing exercise as being every bit as valuable as that $5,000."

You can't start an exercise program that you intend to make permanent without doing a little thinking first. And as Dr. Hill aptly points out, one of the things you need to think about is how to make exercise seem like something you just can't do without.

XAVIER F. PI-SUNYER, M.D.
Columbia University, New York City

"For me, weight control means following a few simple rules," says Dr. Pi-Sunyer. "I walk 20 blocks each way to and from work every day—spring, summer, fall and winter. And at the hospital, I usually don't take the elevator; I take the stairs."

Dr. Pi-Sunyer also makes sure to eat three meals a day, minus the desserts and also minus any snacks in between. "It's not exotic, but it does keep me at my target weight."

DAVID SCHLUNDT, PH.D.
Vanderbilt University, Nashville

When Dr. Schlundt gets ready for work in the morning, he doesn't pop his laptop computer into a briefcase—he pops it into a backpack and then hits the road on his bike. "I'll do anywhere from 3 to 16 miles to and from work, depending on how much time I have and which route I take. It's the perfect way to maintain my weight without giving up a lot of time to do it. I have to commute anyway, so why not do it on my bike?"

Dr. Schlundt eats as much as he needs to. "I'll also do a step aerobics class when I can fit it in, so I need a lot of calories! Calories aren't bad in themselves. They just need to be burned off if you're going to keep your weight down."

—Mark Golin

Take Aim
on a Slimmer Shape

Use our figures to find your perfect weight, based on body mass index. Then firm up and trim down by following the experiences of more than 10,000 Prevention *readers.*

Judging from the tidal wave of low-fat foods washing up on supermarket shelves and the multitude of health clubs popping up on city streets, you'd think that America has become the land of the lean and the home of the fit.

Not quite. Not by a long shot. In fact, the National Center for Health Statistics in Hyattsville, Maryland, reports that one in three Americans is now seriously overweight—the highest number ever. Experts call obesity an epidemic, and it's one that is spawning major health problems. Heart disease, endometrial and possibly breast cancer, high blood pressure, high cholesterol, weakened immunity, gallstones, gout, diabetes, osteoarthritis, stroke and sleep apnea are all associated with overweight.

But do we really know what our healthiest weights are? And how many of us are on target? Most important, we're curious to learn from those who are on target what they're doing differently from those of us who aren't. With this in mind, *Pre-*

COULD SO MANY WOMEN BE WRONG—PERHAPS EVEN OBSESSED WITH THINNESS?

vention magazine surveyed its women subscribers about weight control. Apparently, we hit a nerve, because more than 10,000 women responded.

When the editors opened the envelopes, frustration fairly leaped off the pages of the responses. Ninety percent of the respondents confess they need to lose weight (on average, 27 pounds). Only 14 percent describe themselves as "well-toned," and just 7 percent say they're "very satisfied" with their bodies. More than half admit they're "not very" or "not at all" satisfied.

What's a Healthy Weight?

Surprisingly, by current Metropolitan Life Insurance Company height and weight tables, barely a majority of the respondents—59 percent—fall into the overweight category, a far cry from the 90 percent who profess to be.

Could so many women be wrong—perhaps even obsessed with thinness?

Our survey found scant evidence of this. And when we asked the opinions of the nation's top medical researchers and experts on obesity, they validated our readers' instincts.

"Slimmer is definitely healthier," says William P. Castelli, M.D., medical director of the famed Framingham Heart Study in Massachusetts.

Dr. Castelli and others argue that the MetLife tables, which were revised in 1983 to allow for more weight, have become too lenient. In fact, the American Heart Association has urged people to ignore those guidelines. According to the current MetLife tables, for example, 155 pounds is within the desirable weight range for a five-foot-five woman.

The MetLife tables are based on death rates and vital statistics from millions of insurance holders in the United States. Dr. Castelli points out, however, that they don't account for the fact that many thin people with high death rates are cigarette smokers or otherwise ill. If those people had been eliminated from the current tabulations, he says, the desirable weights would be lower.

Fortunately, researchers are exploring better ways to evaluate optimal body weight based on the latest research on weight-related health risks. Two approaches, used together, are emerging as the new "gold standard" for such evaluations: body mass index and waist/hip ratio.

All about Body Mass Index

Body mass index (BMI) is a ratio of weight to height. It's determined by a mathematical formula. First, you divide your weight (in pounds) by your height (in inches) squared, then multiply the resulting number by 705. You should get a BMI that's somewhere between 19 and 30. If this sounds too complicated, don't worry; we've done the calculations for you. (See "Calculating Body Mass Index" on page 34.)

Several large medical studies, involving thousands of people, have suggested that 21 to 22 is the optimal BMI. At this level, there are no weight-related health risks, Dr. Castelli explains.

One large-scale study that points to a BMI below 22 as ideal for preventing heart disease in women is the Nurses' Health study, based at Harvard University and Brigham and Women's Hospital in Boston. In it, researchers followed 115,886 initially healthy American women, ages 30 to 55, for eight years. During that time, 605 of the women experienced coronary heart disease, leading to 83 deaths. There was no elevated risk of heart disease among women whose BMIs were under 21. The risk was 30 percent higher than

CALCULATING BODY MASS INDEX

To find your body mass index (BMI), locate your height in the left column. (If you've lost inches over the years, use your peak adult height.) Move across the chart (to the right) until you hit your approximate weight. Then follow that column down to the corresponding BMI number at the bottom of the chart.

Height	Body Weight (lb.)						
4'10"	91	96	100	105	110	115	119
4'11"	94	99	104	109	114	119	124
5'	97	102	107	112	118	123	128
5'1"	100	106	111	116	122	127	132
5'2"	104	109	115	120	126	131	136
5'3"	107	113	118	124	130	135	141
5'4"	110	116	122	128	134	140	145
5'5"	114	120	126	132	138	144	150
5'6"	118	124	130	136	142	148	155
5'7"	121	127	134	140	146	153	159
5'8"	125	131	128	144	151	158	164
5'9"	128	135	142	149	155	162	169
5'10"	132	139	146	153	160	167	174
5'11"	136	143	150	157	165	172	179
6'	140	147	154	162	169	177	184
BMI	**19**	**20**	**21**	**22**	**23**	**24**	**25**

that of the lean group for women whose BMIs were between 21 and 25, 80 percent higher for BMIs between 26 and 29 and 230 percent higher for BMIs greater than 29.

"Obesity is a strong risk factor for coronary heart disease in middle-age women," the researchers concluded. "Even

124	129	134	138	143	148	153
128	133	138	143	148	153	158
133	138	143	148	153	158	163
137	143	148	153	158	164	169
142	147	153	158	164	169	174
146	152	158	163	169	175	180
151	157	163	169	174	180	186
156	162	168	174	180	186	192
161	167	173	179	186	192	198
166	172	178	185	191	197	204
171	177	184	190	197	203	210
176	182	189	196	203	209	216
181	188	195	202	207	215	222
186	193	200	208	215	222	229
191	199	206	213	221	228	235
26	**27**	**28**	**29**	**30**	**31**	**32**

mild to moderate overweight is associated with a substantial elevation in coronary risk." Other large-scale studies have reached similar conclusions.

Beyond heart disease and diabetes, there seems to be a broader safety range. A BMI between 23 and 25 isn't ideal, some experts insist, but the excess risk for cancer and other weight-related diseases seems to be small. Roughly around a BMI of 26, these health risks appear to rise, although scientists don't agree on exactly where to draw the line.

"Between 25 and 27 is a gray zone," says Jean Pierre Despres, Ph.D., associate director of the Lipid Research Center at Laval University in St. Foy, Quebec. "A lot of people in this range are perfectly healthy, but others have a substantially higher risk of developing diabetes and premature coronary disease."

Most scientists do agree that a BMI over 27 increases risk for many people. But risk also depends on other factors, including their waist/hip ratios, notes Dr. Despres.

By the BMI method, over three-fourths of our survey respondents weigh more than the optimal (healthiest) weight. At the other end of the scale, 2 percent are underweight.

And what about underweight? Excessive thinness is less common than overweight in the United States. But it is linked with osteoporosis and other health problems, even early death, especially if weight loss is sudden. Most experts feel that people with BMIs under 19 should be evaluated, says James O. Hill, Ph.D., associate director of the Center for Human Nutrition at the University of Colorado Health Sciences Center in Denver. "That doesn't mean everyone that low is going to be unhealthy, but it's worth taking a closer look," he says.

The Rest of the Story

BMI doesn't tell the whole story. Researchers have determined that the fat most associated with health risks is on the upper body—the abdomen and above—rather than on the thighs and hips. (A pattern of upper-body fat is often called central obesity.)

One way to judge whether you have too much upper-body fat is by measuring your waist (at the midpoint between your bottom ribs and hipbone) and your hips (at their widest point). Then divide the waist measurement by the hip measurement. The resulting number is your waist/hip ratio.

This technique, though not perfect (it isn't very reliable for women who are very thin or very overweight, for exam-

> **F**AT THIGHS ARE OKAY. **I**T'S BELLY FAT THAT IS UNHEALTHY.

ple), can in most cases prove very predictive of cardiovascular disease risk, especially in women.

"Central obesity is turning out to be the most lethal risk factor associated with excess body weight," says Dr. Castelli. That's because upper-body fat is strongly correlated with visceral fat, which is fat that's packed around our internal organs.

While more of the research on the health risks of upper-body fat has been done with men, more research with women is beginning. Researchers at the University of Miami School of Medicine and the University of Minnesota School of Public Health in Minneapolis, for example, examined data on 32,898 healthy women ages 55 to 69. In a four-year period, there were nearly three times as many heart disease deaths among women with the greatest waist/hip ratios (over 0.86) as among women with the lowest ratios.

A high waist/hip ratio has also been associated with diabetes, high blood pressure, breast and endometrial cancer and high cholesterol.

What's an ideal waist/hip ratio? While scientists quibble over hundredths of a percent, most target 0.8 or less as desirable for both women and men.

How did our *Prevention* survey respondents do with waist/hip ratio? Better than with BMI. Sixty-two percent have healthy waist/hip ratios. Our readers' average was 0.79. And that's not bad!

Dr. Castelli is one of several scientists who believe that waist/hip ratio is even more important than BMI in predicting risk. "If someone has a healthy BMI but a high waist/hip ratio, it is important to try to bring that waist/hip ratio down," he explains. "Someone with a higher BMI but a low waist/hip ratio might not be quite as bad off."

To help you better evaluate your weight-related health risk, we've developed a scale that integrates BMI and weight/hip measurements. (See "Your Healthy Weight Target.")

Overweight or Overfat?

Considering how our survey respondents measure up on BMI and waist/hip ratio, we still were a bit confused. Sixty-six percent of the women in the optimal range say they feel they need to lose weight.

According to weight-control experts, some people may be confusing overweight with overfat. Maybe many of our "optimal" respondents don't really need to lose pounds—but they do need to lose fat and improve their muscle tone.

Indeed, among those optimal respondents, 31 percent say they are well-toned. That leaves 64 percent who feel they're not—virtually the same percentage as optimals who feel they need to lose weight!

Along with BMI and waist/hip ratio, muscle tone does have relevance to health risks and weight. After all, scientists agree that the danger of overweight generally is not from heavy bone or muscle; it's from excess fat.

Exact standards don't exist for how much body fat a person can carry without increasing risk, but at the Cooper Aerobics Center in Dallas, they aim for 18 to 22 percent of total

Your Healthy Weight Target

To determine whether your body weight is on target or is increasing your disease risk, find your body mass index on the vertical column and your waist/hip ratio on the horizontal line. Now locate the point at which they meet to see if you need to trim some pounds or inches.

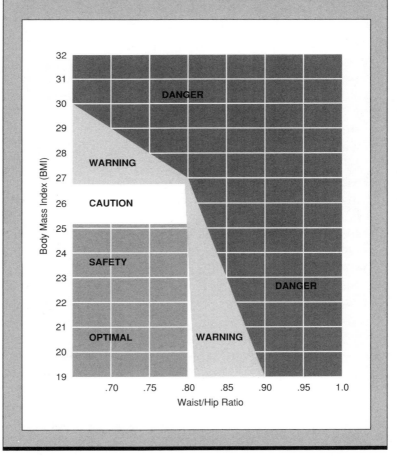

weight for women as optimal, slightly higher than for men.

Unfortunately, it's not easy to determine percentage of body fat. There are a number of ways to go about it, from pinching skin folds with calipers to bioelectric impedance (running a mild current through the body to measure resistance) to underwater weighing. These methods are not widely available outside health clubs and specialists' offices and are not always reliable.

IF YOU LOOK FLABBY, YOU PROBABLY ARE.

An easy way to judge whether you're overfat is by looking in a mirror, says Joan Marie Conway, Ph.D., research chemist at the U.S. Department of Agriculture Human Nutrition Research Center in Beltsville, Maryland. She suggests you simply eyeball it. If you look flabby despite good BMI and waist/hip ratio numbers, you probably are. And you'd do well to embark on an exercise regimen that burns fat and tones muscle.

Through all of the weighing and measuring, it's important not to get too hung up on the scale or measuring tape, she adds. "You could never use one number to tell someone his risk for disease," says Dr. Conway.

Dr. Despres agrees. "There are other factors to consider, too, including family history, good and bad health habits such as smoking and exercising and personal health risks such as high cholesterol, low HDL cholesterol (the good kind) and high blood pressure," he says. "People with more risk factors must be more careful of their weight."

Clearly, finding your perfect weight for health is not yet a precise science. But it's safer to err on the side of slender, says Dr. Castelli. "You may be on the borderline today, but where are you going to be five years from now? Get in the habit of controlling your weight before you have a problem, not after."

How Do You Spell Success?

This brings us to the most interesting of our survey results—that is, how our respondents with optimal weight readings stay slim.

Weight loss isn't so hard for our readers. The toughest challenge, of course, is keeping the weight off. After all, the vast majority of respondents (86 percent) say they've lost six pounds or more, then regained it—some of them dozens of times.

In our survey analysis, we identified those women who are more successful than others at maintaining a healthy weight. We were particularly interested in learning what differentiates their lifestyles.

When we looked at their diets, the women whose weights are optimal seem about equally committed to low-fat, moderate-calorie eating as heavier women. But we did find one dramatic lifestyle difference between them and others: exercise.

Exercise Makes All of the Difference

It's not that our readers are exercise shirkers, but they may need to exercise more. Just 37 percent exercise four times or more a week. But the women whose weight is optimal go the extra mile: 48 percent exercise four times or more weekly.

Experts agree: Excess weight is a long-term health issue, and remedying it may mean stepping up the amount of exercise you get.

"It's known that the only way to maintain weight loss forever is to increase the amount of physical activity you do," says Miriam Nelson, Ph.D., research scientist at the U.S. Department of Agriculture Human Nutrition Research Center on Aging at Tufts University in Boston.

Lack of exercise is a major reason for the rise of obesity in the United States. Between our desk jobs and our automobiles, we don't move our bodies enough to ward off the gain in fat that comes with aging. Problem is, many people may not know that they need to include deliberate exercise in their daily routines.

"People with desk jobs think 'I walk up and down stairs a lot, and I run around doing houshold chores in the evening—I get plenty of exercise.' Even if that adds up to 90 minutes of physical activity, it's not enough," says Dr. Conway. "You need intentional exercise such as fitness walking or cycling to call yourself anything but sedentary."

> **Y**OU NEED INTENTIONAL EXERCISE SUCH AS FITNESS WALKING OR CYCLING TO CALL YOURSELF ANYTHING BUT SEDENTARY.

Indeed, though the respondents of optimal weight are no more active in their daily lives than the overweight respondents, they do participate in more intentional exercise. Overall, many of you (44 percent) exercise for less than a half-hour per session. Yet only 29 percent of women at optimal weight exercise for less than a half-hour. They usually go longer, their workout sessions lasting between a half-hour and an hour. Severely overweight women most commonly report the shortest exercise sessions—less than 20 minutes.

Consistency Is the Key

The survey also found that sticking to an exercise program is a problem for most women but less so for those of optimal weight. Almost two-thirds of all women report trouble with consistency. Just 23 percent say they're "very consistent" about exercise. Meanwhile, of all of the women, 37 percent of the optimal group describe their exercise programs as "very consistent."

To achieve consistency, of course, you must find a form of exercise (or a combination of exercises) that you actually enjoy. "It needs to be something that people like and that they feel they can continue doing indefinitely," says Dr. Hill.

> **E**XERCISE PREVENTS YOUR BODY FROM LITERALLY GOING TO POT AS YOU AGE.

For people at risk from overweight, Dr. Despres recommends walking, walking, walking. The risk of injury is lower than for many other exercises. "We have shown that this is an excellent form of exercise to decrease excess abdominal fat and the complications associated with it," he explains.

"Even if you don't lose a lot of weight, your risk profile will improve with a brisk 45-minute walk four to five days a week," he continues. "If you don't exercise that much, you won't burn enough fat to get the substantial improvement in your risk profile that you'd see with that program."

Exercise prevents your body from literally going to pot as you age. "As people get older, they lose a lot of muscle because of inactivity and poor nutrition," Dr. Nelson explains. "As they lose muscle, their metabolic rates, or energy needs, go down. But they often continue to eat the same amount as they did before. So they accumulate excess fat."

From about their forties, Dr. Nelson estimates, adults lose about 1 percent of their muscle every year. In the meantime, many people gain about a pound of fat a year. But the slide to fat, she adds, really doesn't have to happen if people participate in appropriate physical activity programs that include both some aerobic and some strength-training exercise.

Lift Up Your Health

Which brings us to the other lifestyle habit that differentiates the women of optimal weight from the other women: The optimals do more strength training. Thirty-five percent of those in the optimal group are hefting weights to strengthen muscle, compared with 14 percent or fewer of those in heavier groups.

Why is strength training (with small weights or resistance machines) so important to maintaining a healthy body weight? "Large muscle mass helps burn calories," Dr. Nelson explains. "More muscle means a faster metabolism." That's because muscle requires more oxygen and more calories to sustain itself than body fat does. And strength training is more effective than aerobic exercise in building and maintaining muscle.

When you have more muscle on your body, you burn more calories than someone who doesn't, even when you're both sitting still. So it's easy to understand how people who build muscle have an easier time maintaining a healthy weight. They're more efficient calorie burners.

Another advocate of strength training for healthy, sustained weight loss is *Prevention* fitness adviser Wayne Westcott, Ph.D., national strength-training consultant for the YMCA. "Dieting alone doesn't work. Dieting combined with regular aerobic exercise is better, but it won't replace the muscle tissue that's lost in aging. But when you combine strength training and aerobic exercise with sensible eating, you'll look trimmer, feel more fit and be able to eat more," he explains.

—Cathy Perlmutter with Michele Stanten

Fight Fat
from the Inside Out

Burn fat while you sleep! Think that's a lot of baloney? Well, it's not. Your body's metabolic rate makes the difference. These three easy-to-follow tips will help keep your body's calorie-burning furnace at its hottest.

Ever try to off-load a truck without a ramp? It's murder. Kind of like what many of us go through trying to off-load some body fat and deliver it to oblivion. Every pound seems to require a ton of work.

What if we look for every "ramp" we can find in this weight-loss job? Every dolly? If we're lucky, maybe we can even get hold of one of those hydraulic tailgate jobbos. Anything to make the job easier!

Well, there are leverage devices that do just that. Yes, you still need to work, but you don't need to kill yourself. The idea is to use the body's own calorie ramps, chutes, catapults and other assorted physiological whatnots to help us trim down and stay down.

Our first discovery has to do with something you'll be hearing more and more about: lean body mass. That refers to the percentage of your body that's not fat—muscle, bone and organs. Muscle may be your best-oiled ramp because it works for you 24 hours a day, including Sundays and legal holidays.

YOU COULD LOSE TEN POUNDS OR MORE BY PUTTING ON SOME MUSCLE.

The more relative muscle you have, the higher your calorie burn—every blessed minute of the day. Even when it's not in use, muscle eats up a lot of calories compared with fat. Whereas fat pretty much just lies there, like a storage facility, muscle needs calories to keep it in good repair and ready for action.

And the difference isn't small. You could lose ten pounds or more by putting on some muscle.

Researchers in the Department of Nutrition and Dietetics at King's College, University of London, found that people with relatively more muscle (or lean body mass) were burning more calories even as they fell asleep listening to the radio. Folks who generally exercised at a moderate level for about an hour a day combusted about 8 percent more calories than sedentary people, even on off days. Serious athletic types who trained nearly two hours a day were burning off about 14 percent more calories than the nonexercisers.

This amounts to about 144 calories for the moderate folk (like most of us) and 288 calories for the heavy-duty athletes.

Remember, that's over and above the calories burned while actually exercising, and it's due entirely to having more muscle.

So muscle is about as close to a hydraulic tailgate for unloading fat as you're going to get. To get muscle, get into resistance training. Dumbbells, stretch bands and machines will all do the trick. Combined with walking or aerobics, which burns off lots of calories directly, resistance training will give you the extra lean body mass you need to smoke off flab all day long.

The Alcohol Damper

So here you are with the inner fire of lean body mass. And right over there is the fridge. In goes your arm, and out comes a jug of spring water. Your thirst is slaked. But is your metabolic fire, too?

No way. Water only helps.

But what will slake that fire is a flagon of ale, a pitcher of martinis or a jeroboam of muscatel.

Alcohol, when consumed in addition to a normal diet, actually blocks your body's ability to burn fat for energy. A study pinpoints the extent of this blockage at just about one-third. In one experiment, when alcohol was run directly

> **A**LCOHOL ACTUALLY BLOCKS YOUR BODY'S ABILITY TO BURN FAT FOR ENERGY.

into the body over a period of four hours, the oxidation of fat was reduced by 70 percent! Moral: While you're trying to get fat off your tailgate, don't let alcohol merrily carry it right back on. Go with water.

Pulling the Fat Tooth

We all know that eating a diet high in fat is the Big Neon No-No of weight loss in the 1990s. But aside from the fact that an ounce of fat has more than double the calories of protein or carbohydrates, there's another way that fat actually fouls up your normal ability to keep your belly in check.

Here's why, according to Kevin J. Acheson, Ph.D., of the Nestlé Research Centre in Lausanne, Switzerland. Eat too much protein, and your body gets rid of most of it by burning more protein for energy and pumping it out through the urinary tract. Eat too many carbohydrates, and up goes the inner flame under those potatoes.

FACING A DESSERT OF EITHER A SLICED ORANGE OR A VERY SMALL PIECE OF CHEESECAKE WITH THE SAME NUMBER OF CALORIES, WHICH ONE IS LIKELY TO MAKE YOUR MOUTH GO "SECONDS!"?

In contrast, writes Dr. Acheson, "fat oxidation does not respond rapidly to an increase in fat intake, and fat composition of the body must increase dramatically before a significant increase in lipid (fat) oxidation occurs."

Fat may even resist short-term semistarvation diets. What happens is that your body will keep the fat and instead burn your precious lean body mass to keep itself alive. Horrible, huh?

We got another insight into the leveraging power of a low-fat diet from Xavier F. Pi-Sunyer, M.D., professor of medicine at Columbia University in New York City. Although stressing that total calories is what ultimately tells the story, Dr. Pi-Sunyer says it's also true that "people with high-fat diets tend to overeat, because fat enhances palatability. And as they overeat, they gain weight."

Never thought of that, actually. But it does make sense. Facing a dessert of either a sliced orange or a very small piece of cheesecake with the same number of calories, which one is likely to make your mouth go "Seconds!"? The low-fat alternative works like the low-alcohol technique here: It prevents unnatural weight gain.

But please don't think that because fat "enhances palatability," a low-fat diet is unpalatable. It's a matter of conditioning, research done a few years ago suggests. By following a healthy, low-fat diet, you're quite likely to lose that "fat tooth." In the Women's Health Trial at the Fred Hutchinson Cancer Research Center at the University of Washington in Seattle, many women said that within six months of eating better, they actually found fatty foods unpleasant to eat.

So there we have still another good ramp for unloading unwanted pounds. Build it, and they will go away.

—*Mark Bricklin with Michele Stanten*

Part II
Make It a Habit—For Life

Put Your Life in Motion and Lose Weight

Even if you're not splitting wood, plowing the lower 40 or hanging laundry, you can find ways to add muscle-building, calorie-burning action to the most sedentary lifestyle. So toss out the remote control and get moving! Here's how.

Have you become a certifiable yo-yo? We mean an ever-fluctuating dieter. Summertime you're slim; wintertime you're plump. After a long weekend of weddings and receptions, your belt feels as constricting as a circus snake, and only after a week of intense dieting does it relax. You find, to your dismay, that you no longer need a scale to tell you if you're overweight. Your belly and your belt loops do a fine-enough job without it.

It's time to face the facts: Losing weight requires more than emergency measures such as crash dieting. Such strict tactics, you soon realize, not only make you feel deprived, cranky and hungry, they simply don't work. Crash dieting may do the job short-term, but such unrelenting hardship is virtually impossible to maintain over time.

"For most people, permanent weight loss is better achieved through modest lifestyle changes than through drastic measures," says James O. Hill, Ph.D., associate director of the Center for Human Nutrition at the University of Colorado Health Sciences Center in Denver. These changes, thankfully, can amount to no more than some simple tweakings of how you already live your life. "By reducing sedentary behavior and increasing activity through planned exercise and everyday habits, the weight loss will come—and stay for good," Dr. Hill explains. Research has shown that the best predictor for maintaining weight loss is exercise.

Three Ways to Exercise More

Dr. Hill's approach is simple: While maintaining your caloric intake, increase activity in three key areas of your life. "During the day, you're inactive, taking part in daily activities or engaging in some planned exercise," says Dr. Hill. "By targeting those three areas with small changes, together they can have an enormous impact in terms of weight loss."

Here's how it works. Let's say you want to lose six pounds and keep off the weight for good. "In order to lose that weight, you would have to keep your calorie intake constant and burn off roughly 150 extra calories of energy each and every day," says Dr. Hill. "You would then look at those three areas and figure out where to burn those 150 calories."

First, take a look at the amount of time you spend sitting, watching television and napping—your sedentary time. "By replacing 30 to 40 minutes of inactivity with some leisurely walking, you can increase the amount of energy burned that day by 40 to 60 calories," says Dr. Hill.

Next, take a gander at your routine activities—the time you spend in motion, doing chores such as raking leaves, vacuuming, washing the car, digging in the garden and running errands and going places on foot. "By increasing the amount of daily activities you do—say, taking the stairs instead of the elevator or walking instead of reading the newspaper at lunch—you can easily burn off another 50 calories," says Dr. Hill.

Finally, target your planned daily exercise. By adding an extra 15 minutes to your evening stroll—bam! You've peeled off another 50-plus calories, putting you over the top for your 150-calorie goal. Keep at it, and the six pounds will follow. But be patient—it may take a while.

TO LOSE WEIGHT, SPREAD THE WORK AROUND: A LITTLE LESS SITTING, A FEW HOUSE-HOLD CHORES AND SOME EXTRA WALKING OR JOGGING.

That's just one example of how to follow Dr. Hill's plan for permanent weight loss. By increasing activity in these ways, it may help you permanently lose as much as 25 pounds.

Now you can come up with your own action plan using this special workbook, which is based on the doctor's novel approach. Consider this a perfect start for a slimmer year.

"The workbook features three sections, each one focusing on an area of your life where you can increase activity," says Dr. Hill. And here's where this strategy breaks the mold. To lose weight, just spread the work around however you like: a little less sitting around here, a few household chores there, and some extra walking or jogging at night. "By spreading it around, the commitment isn't as challenging, and you're much more likely to succeed," says Dr. Hill.

Your Weight-Loss Workbook

Whether your weight-loss goal is 5 pounds or 25, check "Move It to Lose It" to determine exactly what you need to do in the calorie-burning department. (The weight-loss

MOVE IT TO LOSE IT

Up your activity ante to burn 150 to 600 additional calories a day, depending on your weight-loss goal.

Weight-Loss Goal (lb.)	Extra Calories to Burn Each Day	Estimated Time (Weeks)
5–6	150	17
10–12	300	20
15–18	450	20
20–25	600	21

goals are to be achieved over one year's time.) Once you pick a realistic goal, read the workbook and decide where this calorie deficit can best fit into your life. "Remember, you don't adapt to this program—it adapts to you," says Dr. Hill. But be realistic. If you have 25 pounds to lose, don't start off by trying to burn the 600 calories needed each day, especially if you have been sedentary for a long time. "Start with a goal of 150 calories per day. Then slowly build on your calorie deficit so that in time, you are burning enough to reach your goal," says Dr. Hill.

Be aware that when you burn more calories than usual, you may very well compensate for some of that burn-off by eating more. "The weight-loss goals are based on the assumption that you may compensate in calories," says Dr. Hill. Translation: If you burn an extra 300 calories a day, you can eat a few extra calories and still hit your goal. But keep in mind that you'll reach your goal more quickly if you don't eat more.

Of course, all of the weight-loss goals can be met more easily if the person trying to lose weight is eating a healthy, low-fat diet, and everyone's goal should be to eat in such a healthy way. But it is possible to reach the first two goals of 5 to 6 pounds and 10 to 12 pounds through exercise alone. Once you shoot for 15 pounds and beyond, though, exercise alone may not be enough to help you reach your goal. It may also help to adhere to a low-fat diet.

Your Sedentary Mode

Sedentary is a nice word for doing nothing. At rest or while sitting, you expend a paltry 50 to 70 calories per hour. If your 9-to-5 job doesn't require much regular movement or you happen to spend a lot of time watching the tube or gabbing on the phone, this may be the area to key in on.

How many hours do you spend at rest (sitting or basically inactive, not counting sleep) throughout the day?

A. More than 5
B. 3 to 5
C. Less than 3

If you selected A, then you're not a couch potato—you're a full-blown sectional sofa. "It's easy to end up like that," says Dr. Hill. "Some people who are sedentary at work or at home during the day and who then watch television at night can easily rack up eight hours of inactivity."

For those folks who are completely inactive, though, there is good news. "You'll have the most to gain, even with just a small change," says Dr. Hill. "Research clearly shows that going from doing almost nothing to doing just a little holds the most potential for improvement in terms of overall health and maybe in terms of weight loss as well."

Your first step, then, is to aim low: Reduce your nonactivity by at least 30 minutes. Then over time, keep chipping away. "By replacing 30 minutes of nothing with 30 minutes of some mild activity, you can burn off an extra 40 to 50 calories or more," says Dr. Hill. Decrease nonactivity by 60 minutes, and you'll burn off 100 calories or more . . . and so on.

"The point is not to replace that inactive time with high-impact aerobics but to simply get moving, even if it's a relaxing walk," says Dr. Hill.

If you chose B, you aren't off the hook. "It still couldn't hurt to knock 30 to 60 minutes off those three to five hours of inactivity," says Dr. Hill. Of course, if your job requires you to stay seated for that amount of time, you may have to create your calorie deficit elsewhere.

> **S**TART WITH A GOAL OF 150 CALORIES PER DAY. THEN SLOWLY BUILD ON YOUR CALORIE DEFICIT SO THAT IN TIME, YOU ARE BURNING ENOUGH TO REACH YOUR GOAL.

If you picked C and spend only three hours or less sitting or resting, you may already lead an active daily life. Create your calorie deficit with either more daily activities, described in the next section, or planned exercise, discussed in the last section.

Your Daily Activities

Getting things done is its own kind of exercise, and just like a robust workout, it burns calories. "Chores, office work, running errands—you can enlist all of them in achieving your weight-loss goal," says Dr. Hill. First, estimate how much time you spend being active during the day by answering the questions below.

1. While you're on the job, how many hours do you spend on your feet and moving throughout the day?
A. 1
B. 2
C. 3
D. 4 or more

2. On average, how many flights of stairs do you climb during a day?
   A. None at all
   B. 1 to 5
   C. 6 to 10
   D. More than 10

3. On average, how many miles do you walk a day (not planned exercise but the walking you do to and from work, in the hallways and running errands)?
   A. ½
   B. 1
   C. 2
   D. 3 or more

4. On average, how many hours do you spend engaging in activities such as gardening, chores and housecleaning during the day?
   A. 1
   B. 2
   C. 3
   D. 4 or more

These questions can give you a good idea of how active you are above and beyond planned exercise. If you walk very little during the day (roughly less than a mile) but engage in one to two hours of strenuous chores, chances are you're already doing pretty well in this department. If so, you can move on to the discussion of planned exercise in the next section. But if you find that you're doing very little of any of the activities mentioned above, then this may be the right spot for running up a calorie deficit. Look over the list of daily activities that follows and try to integrate them into your day. Some are simple little changes, while others require a little more effort.

1. Instead of taking the elevator, take the stairs. The one to two minutes it takes to make it up a couple of flights can burn off 10 to 20 calories. "Two or three trips a day up the stairs—it adds up," says Dr. Hill.

TAKE A ONE-MILE WALK BEFORE YOU EAT. A STROLL CAN BURN OFF ABOUT **100** CALORIES AND MAY DIMINISH YOUR APPETITE.

2. Instead of spending your whole lunch break sitting and eating, take a one-mile walk before you eat. A stroll can burn off about 100 calories and may diminish your appetite. Done five days a week, it can add up to a sizable loss in pounds.

3. If you don't have time for a sustained walk, take brisk mini-walks of five to ten minutes throughout the day. Thirty minutes total each day may burn an extra 150 calories.

4. Pick one part of your house or property that needs spot cleaning, whether it's window cleaning or mopping or scrubbing floors. Your residence may already be spotless, but consider the rewards: Window cleaning, mopping and scrubbing without pause can rack up 250 calories in for one hour's work. Washing dishes can clear off 135 calories per hour, while washing clothes can soak you for 160 calories per hour.

5. Do more standing. Standing for an hour amounts to only a 10- to 20-calorie difference over sitting for an hour, but it can add up. If you find yourself deep in thought, consider using your feet as well as your brain: Pace. For every 15 steps or so, you'll burn a calorie.

6. Instead of driving right to your company parking lot, park a few blocks away and walk the rest of the way. If you walk only one-fifth of a mile, it can burn off 20 to 25 calories. To and from can deflate your day by 50 calories—250 calories for the week, weather permitting.

7. Get down to some serious lawn work: Rake, sack

RATING THE EXERCISES YOU LIKE

Look over the following exercises and rate them on a scale 1 to 10, according to personal preference. The activities are grouped by intensity, or how many calories they burn in an hour.

Activity*	Calories Burned per Hour
MILD TO MODERATE	
___ Walking, 2–2.5 mph	185–255
___ Bicycling or stationary cycling, 5.5 mph	245
___ Golf, walking with clubs	270
___ Aerobics, low-impact	275
___ Ballroom dancing	300
___ Calisthenics	300
___ Rowing (machine), easy	300
___ Strength training	300
___ Table tennis	300
___ Treadmill walking, 4 mph	345
___ Aerobics, medium-intensity	350
___ Horseback riding	350
___ Roller skating	350
___ Square dancing	350
___ Hiking with a 20-pound backpack, 3 mph	400
___ Bicycling or stationary cycling, 10 mph	415
___ Tennis	425

leaves, trim shrubs and trees or cultivate a garden. If you're paying someone to do it for you, then you may also be paying for it by missing out on some easy calorie-burning activity. For example: Pushing a lawn mower burns 350 calories per hour; raking the lawn, 220 calories per hour; and garden work, 250 calories per hour.

Activity*	Calories Burned per Hour
MODERATE TO INTENSE	
___ Polka dancing	540
___ Swimming	540
___ Walking, 5 mph	555
___ Cross-country skiing, 5 mph	600
___ Handball	600
___ Bench stepping, medium-intensity	610
___ Bicycling or stationary cycling, 13 mph	655
___ Rowing (machine), hard	655
___ Running/jogging, 5.5 mph	655
___ Rope jumping	660
___ Stair climbing (machine)	680
___ Running, 7.2 mph	700
___ Martial arts	790

*The number of calories burned by each activity is estimated based on what a 150-pound person might use up in an hour's time.

8. If you are at work and need to reach someone across the building, don't call—stop by his office instead. Reduce your phone calls and substitute person-to-person contact.

Now come up with a few activities of your own. Think about how you spend your day. Jot down some activities that you could add to your daily life that would increase the amount of overall motion and help run up a calorie deficit. Remember, we aren't talking exercise—that comes next. We're talking simple movement. Then try them out.

Your Planned Exercise

So your job keeps you on your toes, and you rarely find yourself sacked out in front of the television watching re-runs. You also engage in a lot of daily activities: schlepping groceries, walking to and from work, tending to your garden. In short, you are one busy beaver. The best place to target your calorie deficit, then, may be in your planned exercise. Answer this question.

How many hours do you spend in planned, continuous exercise (hitting the gym, walking uninterrupted, taking an aerobics class, playing sports and so on) per week?
A. Less than 1
B. 1 to 2
C. 3 to 4
D. 5 or more

If you aren't getting at least three hours of aerobic exercise per week, consider upping the ante.

THE REAL KEY TO EXERCISING REGULARLY IS WHETHER YOU LIKE THE ACTIVITY. CHOOSE ONE THAT GRABS YOUR FANCY.

"The point is to choose an exercise not because of how many calories it burns but because you enjoy it," says Dr. Hill. "We know that the real key to exercising regularly is whether you like the activity. Choose something that grabs your fancy."

Now if your goal is to knock off 150, 300 or 450 calories each day, you can choose one activity to hit the deficit. Or exercise buffet-style: Burn some calories with one activity and some with another.

If you're an experienced exerciser, you can choose moderate to intense calorie-burning exercises. If you're just starting out, stick with the mild stuff—and enjoy yourself.

—*Greg Gutfeld*

How Health Experts Stay in Top Shape

Ever wonder whether the busy professionals who tell us how to stay healthy practice what they preach? From those who do, here's how.

Health experts! Well, we all know that they request nonsmoking rooms in hotels, eat 30-grain bread and call in MedEvac choppers whenever they smell cheeseburgers.

And they've been doing it since before you and I bought our first walking shoes.

But . . . what are they doing differently these days?

I was really curious about that. How have new discoveries changed the habits of the top 2 percent of those in the know? Are we keeping up with them? And—so we might even toy with the idea of beating them at their own game—we also asked them what they were thinking about doing in the future.

Here's what some of them told us.

DONNA E. SHALALA, PH.D.
U.S. Secretary of Health and Human Services

"I'm eating more fruit, and I added another sport—golf. As for stress management," says this member of President Bill Clinton's Cabinet and America's number one health advocate, "I bought a golden retriever."

PETER SCHRAG, M.D.
Medical Director, Metropolitan Life Insurance Company

"These days, I'm more protective of my private relaxation time. I read more. I go for more walks. And I plan regular vacations.

"I decided that if I wasn't going to make my life pleasant, no one else would make my life pleasant. And yes, I enjoy my life more now than I did ten years ago."

Dr. Schrag adds that like you and me, he watches his weight, eats less fat and exercises regularly.

DAVID SATCHER, M.D., PH.D.
Director, Centers for Disease Control and Prevention, Atlanta

Do you ever feel like an overloaded multiple-plug electrical outlet, with so many tasks drawing your energy that you can hardly keep track of them? Many of the high-achievement people we talked with expressed similar feelings, though none of them is ready to start pulling out any plugs. Instead, like Dr. Satcher, who directs one of the world's most respected health organizations, they're into improving their circuitry.

For Dr. Satcher, that means arising at 5:30 A.M., going for a good jog and then "meditating and relaxing." Far from an indulgence, this daily recharge session helps him meet a challenge that's always there: "How can I be a better leader?"

Though the exercise part of this regimen has faithfully been in place for 30 years, the relaxation and meditation components are new.

Also new is "getting more fiber in my diet," says Dr. Satcher. While the long-term benefits are clear, he says this change also "improves my general functioning and how I feel." In fact, he believes that simply feeling better is something health advocates need to stress more when getting their message out to the public.

"As for the future, I want to spend more time relaxing with my wife and other people."

MICHAEL O'DONNELL, PH.D.
Publisher, *American Journal of Health Promotion*

With three degrees, two daughters and one wife, Dr. O'Donnell's schedule is pretty full.

"At the *Journal*, we define optimal health as a balance of physical, emotional, social, spiritual and intellectual health. And lately, I've tried to spend more time on the social component.

"In the community, I devote more time to trying to help underserved populations. With my family, I actually made a written commitment to spend at least a half-hour a day with each of my daughters. That may not sound like a lot, but believe me, there were plenty of days when I didn't take that time because I got home from work too late. Or maybe I would read a book or talk with my wife.

"I've seen a lot of research lately confirming the importance of social networking and support in terms of enhancing life and longevity and reducing disease. So there's academic justification. But what really stimulated me to make changes was my daughters. Lyndsay is in her teens, and as an adolescent, she needs a lot of parenting. And I'd like to màke Allison, my younger daughter, feel close to me, so she'll be open to my parenting when she's in her teens.

"This helps me remember what's important. Yes, work's important, but not as important as family.

"Another change I'm thinking about is getting involved again in competitive swimming, which I gave up when I got too busy. Masters swimming. I love working out hard, and I love the camaraderie of a swim team. It's also something I can do until I'm 80 or 90!"

MARCIA ANGELL, M.D.
Executive Editor, *New England Journal of Medicine*

"I'm in the business of evaluating new research, and I'm very skeptical of new findings and conservative about my lifestyle," says the editor of one of America's most prestigious medical journals.

"But the one change I've made in the past five years is to increase my supplemental calcium. I'm a small woman of northern European ancestry, and studies indicate that women such as myself are more vulnerable to osteoporosis."

KATHIE DAVIS
Executive Director of IDEA: International Association of Fitness Professionals

"About a year ago, my husband, Peter, and I hired a personal trainer to come to the house once a week and coach us in strength training. We are both avid exercisers, but unfortunately, we never did any resistance training at all.

"So we took a room and transformed it into an exercise/family room with a big-screen television. It has worked out fantastically. Four months into it, our son, Jason, who is ten, decided he wanted to start. So he began with very light weights. Then our daughter, Kelli, who is younger, decided she wanted to do it, too, so it has turned into a fun activity that the whole family can do. I think doing things together strengthens the family bonds. That's important.

"Another change is that I began to take a good multivitamin/mineral supplement every day, and I have our kids taking vitamins, too. I believe it helps quite a bit in preventing us from getting sick with the many things the kids bring home from school."

CELSO-RAMON GARCIA, M.D.
Emeritus Professor of Obstetrics and Gynecology, University of Pennsylvania Medical Center, Philadelphia

Dr. Garcia, now in his seventies, was one of the pioneering team that developed the oral contraceptive. Still very active professionally, Dr. Garcia says he looks forward to enjoying old age, which he hopes to accomplish with minimal "crumpling around the edges," as he puts it. To help do this, he has made four dietary changes.

"First, I eat more fiber. (I love cabbage soup!) The fiber helps you stay trim by filling you up with few calories. Beyond that, I think that as you grow older, it is more common to develop constipation or diverticulitis, and fiber helps protect you against both problems.

"Also, as you grow older, you need to become concerned about osteoporosis. Most people think this is a woman's problem, but as a man reaches his sixties and seventies, he also needs nutritional protection. I take a calcium supplement of 1,000 to 1,200 milligrams a day.

"Vitamin C helps people heal better. That original research was done at this hospital many years ago by Isadore Ravdin. I take 1,500 milligrams twice a day.

"As for vitamin E, the evidence about antioxidants is not completely convincing, but it's impressive enough. I think it's worthwhile, and I take 1,000 international units a day."

KATHLEEN DAELEMANS
Executive Chef and Owner, Cafe Kula at the Grand Wailea Resort and Spa, Maui, Hawaii

"Over the past three years, I've made some rather dramatic changes. When I was hired for this job, I was chosen for my gourmet cooking background. Then at the last moment, they said 'Will you do spa food?' And I said 'Spa food? What's spa food?'

"At that time, I was five feet two inches and weighed 200 pounds. Since then, I've lost 75 pounds. I've never yo-yoed, and I'm still losing.

"How did I do it? By using techniques I developed with the help of the spa's nutritionist to serve healthy, low-fat, delicious meals. I also teach these techniques to our guests. The theme is lots of gradual, simple changes that cut down on fat and sugar and emphasize whole grains, vegetables and fruits.

"Of course, I also exercise. My trick for motivating myself is to buy some really great workout outfits. The minute I get home, I put on my exercise gear, and then I find it hard to justify not working out. I may run or go for a power walk. And I always head for someplace beautiful and special. I believe in spoiling myself!"

MICHAEL J. STOCK, PH.D.
Editor-in-Chief, *International Journal of Obesity*

"Switching more toward a vegetarian diet seems to be the way to go, so I'm eating more fruits and vegetables, which means more fiber, less fat.

"As for the future, I'm impressed with the evidence that moderate alcohol consumption may be beneficial. Being British, I'm more of a beer drinker, but I may switch to red wine, which appears to be the most beneficial."

KENNETH MCDONOUGH, M.D.
Corporate Medical Director and Senior Vice-President, Mutual of Omaha

"Last year, I made the decision that we (Mutual of Omaha) should cover Dr. Dean Ornish's heart disease reversal program. At that time, I went on a retreat in California to get more definitive information on the program. In less than a year, I lost 25 pounds—from 180 to 155.

> **I**T OCCURS TO ME THAT FAT IN THE 1990s IS LIKE TOBACCO WAS BACK IN THE 1950s.

"My diet is now vegetarian and very low in fat. It occurs to me that fat in the 1990s is like tobacco was back in the 1950s.

"For the future, I'd like to join a support group to talk about improving my interpersonal skills and connection with other people. That's the program's fourth intervention, the other three being a low-fat vegetarian diet, moderate exercise and yoga or stress management."

—Mark Bricklin with Michele Stanten

The C Factor

For many people, the key to successful weight loss is a consistent walking program. Here, walking expert Rob Sweetgall explains how to make yours a habit, rain or shine.

Why do some people seem to be better than others at weight control? No, I don't mean naturally skinny people. I mean average people who would balloon if they reverted to bad habits. Somehow they seem to avoid the start-and-stop exercise programs and the accompanying weight fluctuations that the rest of us face.

How do they do it? The same way people get to be good at anything: through motivation, commitment and practice. Success at anything doesn't come suddenly. And once it comes, you can't sit back on your duff and be complacent. This is especially true in the game of weight management. If you're seeking the person who will be the most successful at weight loss, don't look for the one who skips a month of workouts, then burns 5,000 calories in a weekend binge of nonstop exercise. Look for the most consistent one.

In my weight-loss seminars, I find that 99 percent of the people I talk with need more consistency. Part of the problem is the short-term, quick-fix mentality so heavily promoted in the diet industry: Lose ten pounds in ten days. Couple this with the frantic pace of stress-filled, no-time-for-exercise living in America, and you have herds of people who want to exercise but just can't seem to stick with it.

> **P**ART OF THE PROBLEM IS THE SHORT-TERM, QUICK-FIX MENTALITY SO HEAVILY PRO-MOTED IN THE DIET INDUSTRY.

How do the consistent few, who have maintained their programs year after year, keep going? Having talked with hundreds of thousands of walkers since 1985, I have discovered seven healthy principles and habits that consistent people live by. Call them the seven Cs. Adopting one of them can significantly improve your chances of success at losing weight. Adopting all of them virtually guarantees it.

1. Enjoy your exercise. Walking is not a dose of medicine you must swallow with your fingers clasping your nose. There is no medical prescription that works for everyone, such as "Do two miles a day at four miles per hour." What if you can't do four miles per hour? What if two miles doesn't suit your style or schedule?

Some experts will tell you to walk in the morning. Others insist you should walk before, not after, meals. I say walk the way you want to walk! What's most important is doing what you like. Just as some of us are extroverts and others are introverts, there are morning people and night people, nature walkers and urban walkers. Some of us are happy walking around a quarter-mile track or a mall forever. Others have to take a different route every day of the week.

Don't be a slave to a prescription. Pick your pace, place, and partner. If you don't enjoy it, what's the point in punishing yourself? Have fun!

2. Log it. How long does it take to write "three miles, 50 minutes, 300 calories"? More than a few seconds? Of course not. Keeping a log is easy and quick, and it keeps you going.

People who faithfully record their efforts develop an inner commitment, a deeper sense of pride—and an honest understanding of their efforts. Keeping a log also taps your vast resources of guilt, one of the best motivators around. It's hard to go a day without writing something in that log and embarrassing to admit that you've missed three days in a row, even if you're admitting it only to yourself.

I record every workout I do. I try to do it immediately after I exercise, because I am quick to forget. If I don't have my logbook with me, I jot the workout on a piece of paper and transfer it later.

What do I record? Anything and everything that means something to me: where and when, the type of workout, the miles and the number of calories I spend. One of my log pages may represent 3,000 calories of physical activity for a week but only about 60 seconds of writing time a day. That's the length of one television commercial. All I can say is that if you log it, you'll stay with it. It works!

3. Do it daily. Walking is healthful. Done moderately, it's not injury causing, exhausting or difficult. So what's stopping you from doing it every day? Look at your other healthy habits. Do you brush your teeth only three days a week? Do you buckle your seat belt only on weekends? Since walking lowers your stress, blood pressure, blood sugar and body fat and enhances your mood, energy and endorphin levels, why not do it daily?

If you're on an every-other-day walking program, it becomes too easy to skip a day, leaving a big void between workouts. Suddenly, you're down to two days. Then it's one day, and soon you're back in the ranks of the sedentary. Good health habits should be part of daily living. If you want an occasional day off, no problem. Take days off for illness or emergencies, as long as you're out there the other 345 days a year.

4. Go for 24-hour recovery. The great pedestrian Edward Payson Weston walked more than 100 miles per day on many occasions. In fact, Weston used to put on walking exhibitions in which he'd walk 100 miles on back-to-back days. Once he walked 550 miles in six consecutive days. Weston was also famous for his powers of recovery. Though many of his events were within days or weeks of each other, he was able to recover in time for the next one.

> **P**EOPLE WHO FAITHFULLY RECORD THEIR EFFORTS DEVELOP AN INNER COMMITMENT, A DEEPER SENSE OF PRIDE—AND AN HONEST UNDERSTANDING OF THEIR EFFORTS.

How many weekend warriors limp into work on Monday after overextending their bodies? If workouts leave you too tired, too sore or too drained, maybe you need to back off to the point at which you, like Weston, can recover quickly. I believe that fitness walkers should be able to fully recover from a workout within 24 hours. This, I know, goes against some common "no pain, no gain" training principles, which demand that you stress a system to make it come back stronger. But I think noncompetitive walkers can make gains in their fitness and strength levels at such a steady, gradual rate that they never need to feel sore or burned out.

5. Mix it up. The problem for some people is that they are too consistent. These people do the same workout day in and day out. By developing such a monolithic approach to exercise, you face two risks: boredom and stagnancy,

How to Form a Habit

- Start each day thinking about when you'll walk that day.
- Schedule your walks in your datebook as you would a doctor's appointment or a visit with a friend—and take the walking appointment every bit as seriously.
- Substitute walking for a less productive activity. If you watch a lot of television, for example, give up some of it and walk instead. You won't miss it.
- Even if time is tight, take a mini-walk of a few minutes.

which will lead you to a fitness plateau and, eventually, to a fitness decline. Fitness is a little like a shark: It always needs to move ahead. As you get more fit, you have to keep increasing the challenge.

To avoid stagnancy, don't do the same X miles in Y minutes. Instead, one day go a little faster on a shorter workout. The next day, relax on a slower, longer-distance walk. Add in a day of interval training (fast-slow-fast-slow alternating intervals). Vary your route. Throw in a few days of other physical activities such as dancing, biking and gardening. (Yes, gardening counts.) So don't get tunnel vision. Take a broad look at your total activity level, and vary your workouts to keep your mind and body fresh.

6. Walk year-round. The change of seasons can sometimes stall an exercise program. Suddenly, you're too hot or too cold or too wet when you walk, and you stop for a few days. That's just long enough to lose your momentum. I've seen people gain six pounds between Thanksgiving and New Year's. They blame rich holiday food, but the real problem is that come winter, we turn into a nation of weather wimps.

Let yourself acclimate through each change of the four seasons. As summer's humidity sets in, you may want to scale back your distance for a few days until you feel comfortable with the weather. Likewise, even if you get outside for only ten minutes of walking on the first bitterly cold night, just do something. Once you get outdoors and start moving, you will feel refreshed. If you can make that first November adjustment to 40°F air, then December's 30° will not seem so harsh. Granted, there may be some extreme days when it's smarter to stay indoors, but don't let the coldest ten days of the year serve as your excuse not to walk the other 80 days of winter.

7. Prioritize. Lack of time is America's biggest excuse for not exercising. But I once heard that the average American spends about half of his lifetime sleeping (24 years) and watching television (13 years). Yet people who exercise for a half-hour three times a week spend only eight months of their lives exercising. By American standards, those are highly active people.

Sure, finding time is a struggle. But I think that if you believe something is critical enough, you put it at the top of your daily to-do list. The only way you are going to make walking a consistent part of your life is to make it a priority. And when all of the distractions and temptations crop up, simply ask yourself one question: What's more important than your health?

—Rob Sweetgall, president of Creative Walking and author of
eight books on walking, including Walking Off Weight

Part III

Your Key to Smart Shopping

Fat or Fiction?

The best way to drop pounds? Cut back on calories from fat. The new food labels can help you pick low-fat foods, but there's still lots of fat hidden in all sorts of foods. Take this quiz to figure out your best low-fat selections.

We're trying to eat less fat. Honest. But does that mean the turkey franks or the "light" beef franks? The tuna salad or the chicken salad? The tortilla chips or the pretzels? That's the tough part. Take this quiz and assess your fat-finding skills. Don't be discouraged if you miss more than you hit. The quiz is tough.

1. Which breakfast has the least fat?
   A. Bagel with cream cheese
   B. Granola with 2 percent low-fat milk
   C. McDonald's Egg McMuffin
   D. Dunkin' Donuts glazed yeast ring

2. Which two chicken parts have the most fat? (Assume that you eat equal servings of each.)
   A. Breast
   B. Thigh
   C. Wing
   D. Drumstick

3. Order the following cookies from least to most fat.
   A. Chocolate chip
   B. Chocolate sandwich (such as Oreos)
   C. Oatmeal
   D. Fruit-filled bars (such as Fig Newtons)

4. Which of these Italian entrées is lowest in fat?
   A. Fettuccine Alfredo
   B. Lasagna
   C. Spaghetti with meatballs
   D. Eggplant parmigiana with a side of spaghetti

5. Two percent low-fat milk is low in fat.
   A. True
   B. False

6. Which of the following Chinese takeout entrées contains almost a day's worth of fat?
   A. Szechuan shrimp
   B. Chicken chow mein
   C. General Tsao's chicken (orange chicken)
   D. Shrimp with garlic sauce
   E. All of the above

7. Which lunch-counter sandwich has the least fat?
   A. Ham
   B. Chicken salad
   C. Tuna salad
   D. Chicken roll

8. Which hot dog contains at least seven times more fat than any of the others?
   A. Hormel Light & Lean 97 beef franks
   B. Healthy Choice beef franks
   C. Mr. Turkey bun-size turkey franks
   D. Oscar Mayer Healthy Favorites franks

9. Removing the skin from your roasted chicken breast or drumstick can cut the fat by:
   A. One-fourth
   B. One-half
   C. Three-fourths

10. Which one of the following Mexican dinners contains less than a day's worth of fat?
   A. Chicken taco platter
   B. Chicken burrito platter
   C. Taco salad
   D. Cheese enchilada

11. Light or reduced-calorie salad dressings always have less fat than regular dressings.
   A. True
   B. False

12. Which of the following foods has the most fat?
   A. McDonald's Big Mac
   B. ½ cup of Häagen-Dazs ice cream
   C. McDonald's chef's salad with a packet of ranch dressing
   D. Sirloin steak (Select grade), untrimmed

13. Which of the following is highest in fat? Four ounces of:
   A. Round steak (Select grade), untrimmed
   B. Pork tenderloin (Select grade), untrimmed
   C. Chicken thigh, with skin
   D. Sirloin steak (Select grade), untrimmed

14. On average, which line of frozen dinners is lowest in fat?
   A. Healthy Choice
   B. Weight Watchers
   C. Lean Cuisine
   D. Budget Gourmet Light & Healthy

15. Dry-roasted nuts contain about the same amount of fat as regular (oil-roasted) nuts.
   A. True
   B. False

16. Four ounces of Healthy Choice extra-lean ground beef contains four grams of fat. How many grams of fat does four ounces of regular ground turkey contain?
   A. 5
   B. 10
   C. 15
   D. 20

17. Order these salty snacks from least to most fat.
   A. Tortilla or vegetable chips
   B. Corn chips
   C. Light potato chips
   D. Pretzels
   E. Light microwave popcorn

18. Which one of these canned or dried soups has about three times the fat of the others?
   A. Ramen noodle
   B. Split pea with ham and bacon
   C. Chunky beef
   D. New England clam chowder

19. Tablespoon for tablespoon, which are the two lowest-fat toppings for baked potatoes?
   A. Bacon bits
   B. Butter
   C. Sour cream
   D. Light margarine

20. A Burger King BK Broiler grilled chicken sandwich has more than twice as much fat as a McDonald's McGrilled Chicken Sandwich.
    A. True
    B. False

Answers

1. D—Its nine grams of fat aren't really low (or healthy), though. Try a bagel with a tablespoon of light or nonfat cream cheese or a low-fat cereal such as Wheaties with skim or 1 percent low-fat milk.

2. B and C—Dark meat (as long as you're talking drumsticks) isn't always fatty. The white meat on wings is, though.

3. D, C, B, A—Nonfat cookies by Archway, Entenmann's and others are your best choice.

4. C—Spaghetti with red or white clam sauce, tomato sauce or meat sauce is even lower in fat.

5. B—The five grams of fat per glass flunks the Food and Drug Administration's limit for low-fat (three grams). Only skim and 1 percent milk qualify.

6. C—The others have half as much or less.

7. D—The tuna and chicken salads wouldn't be so fatty if you made them with reduced-fat mayo. The leanest meat for your sandwich is turkey breast or chicken breast.

8. C—It has 11 grams of fat; the others have 1 to 1½ grams. In general, though, regular turkey or chicken franks have about one-third less fat than regular beef or pork franks. (Unfortunately, all hot dogs are salty.)

9. B—If you skin the fattier thigh, you'll cut the fat by about one-third.

10. A—But that's only because tacos are small and generally aren't served with guacamole and sour cream.

Even so, a taco platter uses up two-thirds of your day's fat allowance.

11. B—While they usually have less, that's not always the case. Two tablespoons of Ken's Steak House light honey-mustard dressing, for example, contains nine grams of fat. Henri's regular honey-mustard dressing contains just six grams.

12. C—The 30 grams of fat use up almost half of your day's quota. If you get it with the light vinaigrette dressing, the fat plummets to 11 grams (and the saturated fat drops from 7 to 4 grams).

13. C—Even if you skin the chicken, you'll end up with more than twice the fat of the tenderloin, which is one of the few low-fat cuts of pork.

14. A—Healthy Choice dinners average just 14 percent of calories from fat. The others range from 22 to 25 percent. Healthy Choice is also a tad lower in sodium.

15. A—Nuts are so fatty that they don't absorb much extra oil when roasted.

16. C—Regular ground turkey includes fatty skin. Ground turkey breast is as low in fat as the Healthy Choice ground beef.

17. D, E, C, A, B—An ounce of pretzels has just one gram of fat. Then come light microwave popcorn (two to four grams), light potato chips (six grams), tortilla or vegetable chips (seven to nine grams) and corn chips (eight to ten grams).

18. A—Companies such as Campbell Soup, Nissin Foods U.S.A. and Maruchan fry their ramen noodles in fat— often (saturated) palm oil—before their soups are dehydrated.

19. A and C—They have just a couple of grams of fat. A tablespoon (three pats) of light margarine has 6 grams. Butter has 11 grams.

20. A—It wouldn't have been true last year, but sneaky Burger King went and tripled the fat without telling anybody.

What's Your Score?

Give yourself one point for each correct answer on this very tough quiz.

If you scored:

___ *17 to 20*. Fantastic! Even we didn't do this well when we proofread the test.

___ *13 to 16.* Hubba hubba! Congrats. You're the fat champ of your block.

___ *9 to 12.* C-o-o-l! Most people who've taken this test scored in this range. You're on the right track.

___ *5 to 8.* Pretty lean! But room for improvement.

___ *Below 5*. Blubber City! Keep your cardiologist's beeper number in your wallet.

—Jayne Hurley

Hidden Sugar Revealed

Americans consume ten pounds of sugar a month—and most of it doesn't come from cookies and other bad stuff. It's hidden in good foods such as rice cakes and frozen dinners.

Remember all of the wonderful things that you wanted and that your mother kept saying were bad for you—chocolate, sex, Elvis Presley movies, tight blue jeans and sugar, to name a few? Well, the only one that we know for sure she was right about is sugar. It has lots of empty calories. That means it tastes good, rots your teeth, makes you fat and does nothing for your health. Yet despite your mom's worries and the Food and Drug Administration's efforts to reduce your consumption of it, sugar has become the leading ingredient added to foods, largely because it is an inexpensive replacement for fat and salt. "The average person eats five pounds of sugar every two weeks," says Felicia Busch, R.D., a registered dietitian in St. Paul, Minnesota, and a spokesperson for the American Dietetic Association. "It's everywhere, hidden in a lot of foods, from ketchup to salad dressing to low-calorie frozen meals."

When the Whole Pack Becomes Your Snack

Ever scarf down an entire package of a low-fat or nonfat snack in one or two sessions? I have! And so have lots of others, from what I'm hearing. Do that too many times (I did), and pretty soon, you accumulate a few excess pounds. Because these tempting snacks are so low in fat, I think we let ourselves believe that the law of calorie reality (3,500 excess calories equals one pound) is temporarily suspended. That allows the Snack Monster that lives in all of us (even registered dietitians) to take over.

What has helped me get back in control and enjoy low-fat snacks one serving at a time? Calculating the whopping calorie total each time I polish off a whole package of one of my favorites. If you're having the same problem, take a deep breath and focus for a minute on the table to the right. I think it will help!

Though sugar, which is a carbohydrate, does not directly cause any ailment other than tooth decay, research indicates that excess sugar consumption prompts the body to oversecrete insulin, which over time may severely disrupt carbohydrate metabolism and lead to diabetes. But this would require a lot of sugar over an extended period of time. The most common side effects are pretty obvious. Eat too much sugar, and you'll find yourself on an emotional roller coaster, with bursts of energy followed by stretches of lethargy as your insulin level rises and falls.

While 55 percent of your total daily calories should come from carbohydrates, no more than 10 percent of those should come from sugar, according to Franca Alphin, R.D.,

CALORIE REALITY CHECK

Snack	Calories If You Eat One Serving	Calories If You Eat the Whole Package
Nonfat caramel corn cakes	50 (1 cake)	700 (about 6½-oz. pack)
Nonfat chocolate cookie	50 (1 cookie)	600 (6½-oz. box)
Nonfat fig bars	100 (2 cookies)	1,200 (12-oz. pack)
Low-fat tortilla chips	110 (22 chips)	770 (7-oz. bag)
Pretzel chips	120 (16 chips)	1,080 (8½-oz. box)
Reduced-fat mini cheese crackers	130 (38 crackers)	650 (5½-oz. box)
Reduced-fat mini chocolate chip cookies	130 (13 cookies)	910 (7½-oz. box)

nutrition director of the Duke University Diet and Fitness Center in Durham, North Carolina. In an 1,800-calorie diet, that would amount to 990 calories from carbohydrates and only 99 calories (25 grams) from sugar, about what's in one bottle of Snapple iced tea.

The new food labels provide some opportunity to evaluate the sugar content of products. But there is a loophole in the food-labeling law that allows manufacturers to list only simple sugars. Complex, or long-chain, sugars—which make up two-thirds of

THE AVERAGE PERSON EATS FIVE POUNDS OF SUGAR EVERY TWO WEEKS.

WHERE'S THE SUGAR?

Besides the obvious sources, you'll find it in these foods.

Product	Total Calories
Campbell's tomato soup, 4 oz.	100
Dannon Fruit on the Bottom low-fat apple-cinnamon yogurt (99% fat-free), 8 oz.	240
Dannon Light nonfat cappuccino yogurt, 8 oz.	100
Fig Newtons (fat-free), 2	100
Healthy Choice chicken broccoli Alfredo frozen dinner, 1	370
Heinz tomato ketchup, 1 Tbsp.	15
Kraft Free Thousand Island dressing, 2 Tbsp.	45
Nestlé's Sweet Success diet plan, 1 can	200
Pepsi, 1 can	150
Power Bar, 1	225
Quaker banana crunch rice cake, 1	50
Ragu Chicken Tonight light honey-mustard chicken sauce, 4½ oz.	60
Shake'N Bake tangy honey glaze, ⅛ packet	45
SnackWell's devil's food cookie cake, 1	50
Snapple all-natural peach-flavored iced tea, 8 oz.	110
Ultra Slim Fast chocolate fudge, 11 oz.	220
Van Camp's pork and beans, 4½ oz.	110
Weight Watchers Breakfast-on-the-Go blueberry muffin, 1	190

the sugar in corn syrup—are listed under "Total Carbohydrate," even though they break apart into simple sugars during digestion. Be wary of any product with sugar listed in the first four ingredients, says New York City diet psychologist Stephen P. Gullo, Ph.D. And while you're

| Sugar Content | | % Calories |
(g.)	(tsp.)	from Sugar
10	2	40
45	9½	75
13	2¾	52
15	3	60
35	7½	38
4	¾	100
6	1¼	53
30	6⅓	60
41	8¾	100
14	3	25
5	1	40
8	1¾	53
6	1¼	53
9	2	72
26	5½	95
28	6	51
7	1½	25
22	4¾	46

studying the label, keep in mind that sugar goes by many names: dextrose, sucrose, glucose, honey, corn sweetener, brown sugar, fructose, dextrin, high-fructose corn syrup, lactose, modified cornstarch, maltodextrin, maltose, malt, fruit juice concentrate, molasses, mannitol, maple syrup, turbinado sugar, sorghum, xylitol and sorbitol. Whew!

Finally, to roughly translate the sugar grams on the label into teaspoons, divide the number of grams by 4.7. You'll be surprised how quickly the sugar adds up. For instance, there's more sugar than protein in a Healthy Choice chicken broccoli Alfredo frozen dinner: 35 grams of sugar to 23 grams of protein. That's more than seven teaspoonfuls of sugar. Kellogg's Bran Buds cereal sounds so virtuous, but at eight grams of sugar per ⅓ cup, it's not. It contains nearly two teaspoonfuls of sugar, even if you don't add any yourself.

—*Michele Meyer with Holly McCord, R.D.*

What's in a Label?

The new food labels are easier to read, no doubt about that. And we can use them to steer clear of unwanted fat and calories. Here's how to make the most of them.

Have you seen them? No more squinched-to-gether, teeny type, all in hard-to-read capital letters. No more fantasy serving sizes and unexplained grams or milligrams that mean zilch to non-chemists. No more cherry red letters on strawberry red backgrounds.

The new labels are—hang on to your bifocals—legible!

Oh, sure, they'll take some getting used to. Things aren't where they used to be (or they're missing), and that "% Daily Value" is sure to confuse some folks at first. What's more, the new rules don't eliminate all of our friendly food-sellers' tricks.

First, let's walk through a typical label. We've numbered the key facts from most to least important. That way, if your eyes glaze over after the first couple of numbers, at least you'll have hit the high points.

If you're a little depressed about having to learn something new, just think about these benefits.

WHAT'S IN A LABEL?

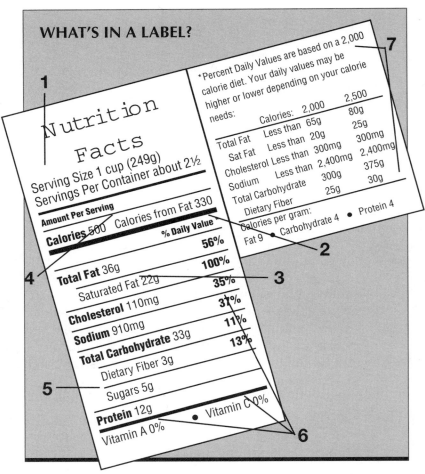

- All of the misleading claims you no longer have to wade through, such as "90 percent fat-free" on high-fat foods or "low cholesterol" on high–saturated fat foods
- How nice it is to have labels include the nutrients you're concerned about, such as saturated fat and fiber
- How nice it is to finally have nutrition information on almost all foods

Best of all, you can read the darned things.

1. Serving Size. Always check the serving size first. It may be a bore, but if you eat less or more than what's listed, you'll have to adjust the other numbers accordingly. Bonus: Serving sizes on the new labels are more realistic.

2. % Daily Value. This tells you how much of a day's worth of fat, sodium and other nutrients that the food provides. For example, this food's 36 grams of fat use up 56 percent of your daily limit, or Daily Value, for fat.

But don't assume that a food has to have 40 or 50 percent of the Daily Value for fat (or whatever) to be high. People eat 15 to 20 foods a day. Our advice: If a food has 20 percent or more of the Daily Value, it's high in that nutrient. Low means no more than 5 percent.

3. Saturated Fat. Check the % Daily Value for saturated fat. It's the nutrient that causes the most damage to health. Just keep in mind that cholesterol-raising trans-fat isn't counted as saturated fat (it's included only in total fat). So if the food contains partially hydrogenated oil, the label underestimates how much it will raise your cholesterol.

4. Calories from Fat. This helps you see how fatty a food is. For example, 330 of 500—or 66 percent—of this food's calories come from fat. Yuk!

5. Sugars. The Food and Drug Administration has refused to set a Daily Value for added sugars because health authorities haven't set a limit on how much we should eat. We recommend 50 grams or less a day.

Unfortunately, the sugars number isn't very precise. It includes naturally occurring fruit and milk sugars. And it omits some of the long-chain sugars that comprise up to two-thirds of some corn syrups.

6. Good guys vs. bad guys. For the first time, you can compare the % Daily Value for "good" nutrients (vitamins A and C, calcium, iron and dietary fiber) with the % Daily Value for "bad" nutrients, such as fat and sodium. With the good guys ranging from 0 to 20 percent of the Daily Value

More Fat Than Meets the Eye

"No cholesterol," boasts the label. Swell. Sounds like this stuff won't raise your blood cholesterol one iota.

Wrong.

Some packaged foods, especially baked goods such as cookies and crackers, are made with partially hydrogenated oil. That means they contain trans-fatty acids. The Food and Drug Administration (FDA) doesn't count trans-fat as saturated, although consumer activists have asked it to.

The FDA has wisely limited the saturated fat in foods that make "no cholesterol" claims to no more than two grams per serving. But if you add this food's trans-fat to its saturated fat, it has three grams of artery-clogging fat.

Until the FDA starts treating trans-fat as saturated, assume that the saturated fat number is an underestimate in foods that are made with partially hydrogenated oil. How much of an underestimate you usually can't tell, but here are some tips.

- If the food is labeled "low-fat," there's too little trans-fat to worry about.
- If a label lists monounsaturated fat and polyunsaturated fat as well as saturated fat, you can add the three and subtract them from the total fat to get a rough estimate of how much trans-fat the food contains. (It's a rough estimate, because the numbers have probably been rounded.) In this case, one serving—equal to three cookies—has about two grams of trans-fat.

and the bad guys ranging from 35 to 100 percent, this food's a loser.

7. *Percent Daily Values chart.* Interesting but not important to check, because it's the same on all labels.

—Bonnie Liebman

Nutrition

Facts

Serving Size 3 cookies (33g)
Servings Per Container about 14

Amount Per Serving

Calories 160   Calories from Fat 60

% Daily Value *

Total Fat 7g   **11%**

Saturated Fat 1.5g   **8%**

Polyunsaturated Fat 0.5g

Monounsaturated Fat 3g

Cholesterol 0mg   **0%**

Sodium 220mg   **9%**

Total Carbohydrate 23g   **8%**

Dietary Fiber 1g   **3%**

Sugars 13g

Protein 2g

Vitamin A 0%   •   Vitamin C 0%

Calcium 0%   •   Iron 4%

*Percent Daily Values are based on a 2,000 calorie diet. Your daily values may be higher or lower depending on your calorie needs:

	Calories:	2,000	2,500
Total Fat	Less than	65g	80g
Sat Fat	Less than	20g	25g
Cholesterol	Less than	300mg	300mg
Sodium	Less than	2,400mg	2,400mg
Total Carbohydrate		300g	375g
Dietary Fiber		25g	30g

Calories per gram:

Part IV

What You Need to Know about Nutrition

The Brave New World of Food Science

Fat substitutes! Aspartame! Fruit punch fortified with vitamin C! In a country dedicated to the pursuit of happiness, people want triple bacon cheeseburgers on sourdough buns, peanut butter fudge ice cream—and slim figures. That's where science comes in.

Americans have always been funny about food. The Pilgrims weren't crazy about the native-grown corn and squash and the wild turkey that were immortalized in that first Thanksgiving. So they tried to plant English seeds, which promptly withered and died. As the country grew and prospered and more citizens had more food choices available to them than any people in history, Americans stuck to a monotonous diet of salted meats, dried beans, cornmeal and potatoes. By the late nineteenth century, John Harvey Kellogg, M.D., saw a nation suffering from dyspepsia, ulcers and chronic fatigue. Although he advocated eating fresh fruits and vegetables, his most famous invention, breakfast cereal, soon became the first big food fad in this country. And Dr. Kellogg's proselytizing turned its consumption into a veritable religion.

Things haven't progressed very far since Dr. Kellogg's day. Americans still tend to confuse nutrition and religion (it's no coincidence that rich desserts are described as "tempting," "decadent" and "sinful"). They feel virtuous when they're dieting. But the puritan urge toward self-denial is at war with the American sense of entitlement. In a country where the prevailing view is that you can be whatever you want to be, it's easy to see why people want to be slim *and* self-indulgent with food.

That's where science comes in.

Throughout American history, the men in the white lab coats have come to the rescue in a pinch. In the nineteenth century, they figured out how to refine, process and preserve foods. When it turned out that refining, processing and preserving eliminated a lot of nutrients, their twentieth-century colleagues figured out how to replace the nutrients in foods artificially.

Today, science faces another nutritional crisis. Never before have Americans been fed so abundantly. Unfortunately, abundance has meant an alarmingly high consumption of fat, cholesterol and sugar and a caloric intake that has made the American derriere an object of wonder around the world. In the early 1990s, one in three Americans was overweight, up from one in four a decade earlier.

What to do? Well, the commonsense answer is to eat smaller portions and to increase the percentage of grains and fresh fruits and vegetables in relation to foods that are loaded with fat and cholesterol. It's hard to change eating habits, though, and that's why science has become the mediator between our desire for high-fat, sugar-laden foods and good nutrition. If we can't change the national "fat tooth," we can at least fool it. Want sweets? Just use lower-calorie, laboratory-designed saccharin and aspartame, which mimic high-calorie natural sugar. Love that butter? Replace natural oils and lard with fat substitutes, and you can keep fatty foods in your diet. Crave gooey snacks and
(continued on page 102)

The Commonsense, All-You-Need Diet

No one has the time to prepare foods from scratch, like our mothers did. Besides, that kind of diet is too high in fat—almost 40 percent of calories. Today, most doctors recommend the government-approved 30 percent, a compromise between reality and the 10 to 20 percent that many nutritionists advocate.

Common sense means going with something you can actually live with. We say that's a moderate 2,000 calories or so, of which 20 percent are derived from fat. The total calories may seem high, but the figure simply recognizes the fact that most people—even ones who say they're dieting—consume at least 1,900 to 2,000 calories a day.

Calcium-fortified orange juice. Of course, fresh orange juice has more antioxidants than the packaged kind, and it tastes better. But for most of us, it's not an everyday affair. Adequate daily calcium is a critical problem for many people, women in particular. The calcium added to packaged orange juice is significant and easily used by the body.

Total cereal. The vitamins and minerals in many breakfast cereals help many Americans reach their Daily Values. Total is a particularly good example of an enriched cereal that is low in sugar.

Fruits and veggies. Bananas and carrot sticks and broccoli and potatoes and romaine lettuce and strawberries: Yes, it's possible to take their chemically active compounds and put them into pills. But beta-carotene or phytochemicals or flavonoids in a jar from a health food store probably will never be as good for you as those in real carrots and broccoli. The same holds for the minerals in potatoes and the antioxidants in romaine lettuce and strawberries.

Rice cakes. Rice cakes are heaven's gift to dieters who love carbs and crunch. Even the contrived flavors, whether they be very sweet (honey spice) or salty (hot salsa), seem to suit them remarkably well. And rice cakes are neater than popcorn.

Breakfast

8 ounces calcium-fortified orange juice
1½ ounces Total cereal
8 ounces 1 percent low-fat milk

Snack

8 ounces low-fat fruit yogurt
1 banana

Lunch

Tuna sandwich made with 2½ ounces water-packed tuna and 1 tablespoon light mayonnaise on whole-wheat bread
Carrot sticks
6 ounces cranberry juice
2 Fig Newtons

Snack

2 rice cakes
1 apple
Iced tea with lemon (no sugar)

Dinner

5 ounces grilled skinless chicken breast with salsa
1 cup steamed broccoli with fresh lemon juice
1 baked potato with 1 tablespoon reduced-fat margarine
Salad: romaine lettuce with 1 tablespoon olive oil and a dash of balsamic vinegar
½ cup vanilla ice milk
½ cup strawberries

Totals: 2,130 calories, 48 grams fat (20 percent of calories), 60 percent of calories from carbohydrates, 20 percent of calories from protein, 190 milligrams cholesterol, 32 grams fiber, 1,775 milligrams sodium, 176 grams sugar.

sweet drinks? Treat them as vitamin supplements by consuming those that have been fortified with double doses of
nutrients. The trouble with products such as Double C
Hawaiian Punch and cookies with added vitamin E, however, is that they may promote the kinds of eating habits
that make the added vitamins necessary in the first place.

Nutritious Double-Fudge Brownies?

These breakthroughs are only the beginning; the most
audacious moves lie just over the horizon. Every day,
biotechnologists are developing new ways to take what is
good about one food and impart it to another. If they can
isolate the elements in plants that are believed to prevent
disease, for example, they can produce entirely new kinds
of foods that lower the risk of contracting certain illnesses.
Perhaps all of this scientific knowledge could be consoli-
dated into a nonfat, calorie-free, vitamin-rich double-fudge
brownie, allowing consumers, at long last, to have their
cake and eat it, too. Welcome to nutritional la-la land.

In the real world, the here and now, life is a bit more
complicated, as the struggle on the fat frontier shows. Scientists have been trying for more than 20 years to create a
substance that reproduces the seductive taste qualities of
fat. Their search took on added urgency in 1988, when the
Surgeon General recommended that Americans reduce
their intake of fat—typically about 40 percent of calories—
to 30 percent. Virtually overnight, fat became Public Enemy
Number One in the national diet drama, which has always
thrived on clearly drawn heroes and villains. In 1984, only
about 8 percent of Americans surveyed said that fat was
their primary worry when purchasing foods. Today, that
figure has jumped to 60 percent.

The food industry responded with a blitz of low-fat and

nonfat products: tofu hot dogs, Milky Ways made with a fat substitute called Caprenin, McDonald's hamburgers slimmed down with water and seaweed extract. But the runaway success story has been Nabisco's SnackWell's line of low-fat and nonfat, cholesterol-free cookies, introduced in the summer of 1992 and now the top-selling cookie in America. The line is so popular that the company cannot bake its nonfat devil's food cookie cake fast enough to keep up with consumer demand. In desperation, fans have formed cooperatives with other SnackWell's customers. Members who spot the cookie cakes agree to buy all of them and then distribute them equally to the other members of the group.

There's a catch, though. When fat goes, something else has to replace it. A SnackWell's cookie sheds all or most of its fat, but it adds flour, nonfat oils and extenders, all of which have calories. This is true of any low-fat or nonfat product. The SnackWell's devil's food cookie cake has the same number of calories as an Oreo—50. Yet some consumers take "nonfat" as an invitation to gorge. Overall, the nation's fat intake has decreased somewhat since the 1960s and 1970s, but its consumption of calories—not to mention nonfat oils and extenders, whatever they are—is on the rise.

> **S**OME CONSUMERS TAKE "NONFAT" ON A PRODUCT AS AN INVITATION TO GORGE.

"I have had several clients who really do eat very low fat, but they consume a lot of those nonfat chocolate-covered, cream-filled mini-cakes," says Francine Grabowski, R.D., a nutritionist at Hahnemann University Hospital in Philadelphia and co-author of *Low-Fat Living for Real People*. "People don't want to believe that they can't eat as much of this stuff as they want."

How Much Fat Do You Eat?

We try to follow commonsense diets and read food labels. Still, it's hard—if not impossible—to tally fat grams every day. What about the fast-food quesadilla for lunch? Or the chicken sandwich?

Researchers at the Fred Hutchinson Cancer Research Center in Seattle have found a way to make the task easier—and to help you with specific fat-fighting strategies as well. A study of women who kept detailed food diaries and then took this quiz indicated that the quiz is a very accurate gauge.

So get your pencil and calculator ready, and begin.

Thinking of your diet over the past three months, complete each of the following items with a number. If an item doesn't apply to your diet, skip to the next one.

1 = Always/usually
2 = Often
3 = Sometimes
4 = Rarely/never

In the past three months:

____ 1. When I ate bread, rolls, muffins or crackers, I ate them without butter or margarine.

____ 2. When I ate cooked vegetables, I ate them without butter, margarine, salt pork or bacon fat.

____ 3. When I ate cooked vegetables, they were cooked by a method other than frying.

____ 4. When I ate potatoes, they were cooked by a method other than frying.

____ 5. When I ate boiled or baked potatoes, I ate them without butter, margarine or sour cream.

____ 6. When I ate green salads, I ate them without dressing.

____ 7. When I ate desserts, I ate them without cream or whipped cream topping.

___ 8. When I ate spaghetti or noodles, I ate the pasta plain or used a meatless sauce.

___ 9. My main meal for the day was meatless.

___ 10. When I ate fish, it was broiled, baked or poached.

___ 11. When I ate chicken, it was broiled or baked.

___ 12. When I ate chicken, I removed the skin.

___ 13. When I ate red meat, I trimmed off all of the visible fat.

___ 14. When I ate ground beef, I chose extra-lean.

___ 15. When I drank milk, I chose skim or 1 percent low-fat instead of 2 percent low-fat or whole.

___ 16. When I ate cheese, it was a reduced-fat variety.

___ 17. When I ate a frozen dessert, it was sherbet, ice milk or a nonfat version of ice cream or yogurt.

___ 18. When I ate green salads with dressing, I used a special low-fat or nonfat dressing.

___ 19. When I sautéed or pan-fried foods, I used a no-stick spray instead of oil, margarine or butter.

___ 20. When I used mayonnaise or a mayonnaise-type dressing, I used a special low-fat or nonfat variety.

___ 21. When I ate dessert, I ate only fruit.

___ 22. When I ate a snack, it was raw vegetables.

___ 23. When I ate a snack, it was fresh fruit.

Scoring

To estimate the overall percentage of calories from fat in your diet, transfer the numbers above to the score sheet on page 106. Figure your average score for each of the five strategies, then average those averages to get your overall score. Then check the chart.

(continued)

How Much Fat Do You Eat?—Continued

Strategy 1. Avoid fat as a flavoring.

___ 1.	___ 6.
___ 2.	___ 7.
___ 3.	___ Subtotal
___ 4.	___ Average*
___ 5.	

Strategy 2. Minimize meat.

___ 8.	___ Subtotal
___ 9.	___ Average*

Strategy 3. Modify meat.

___ 10.	___ 14.
___ 11.	___ Subtotal
___ 12.	___ Average*
___ 13.	

Strategy 4. Substitute low-fat or nonfat versions.

___ 15.	___ 19.
___ 16.	___ 20.
___ 17.	___ Subtotal
___ 18.	___ Average*

Are Low-Fat Foods Helping People Lose Weight?

Replacement fats, developed at enormous cost and launched with great fanfare, are still looking for a break-through hit. Simplesse, a protein-based fat replacement made by the NutraSweet Company, was introduced in 1990 and soon found its way into hundreds of products, notably Simple Pleasures frozen desserts.

Strategy 5. Replace fat foods with produce.
___ 21.   ___ Subtotal
___ 22.   ___ Average*
___ 23.

Total all of the averages and divide by five.
___ **Your Score**

If Your Score Is	Your Percentage of Calories from Fat Is
1 to <1.5	<25
1.5 to <2	25 to 29
2 to <2.5	30 to 34
2.5 to <3	35 to 39
3 to <3.5	40 to 44
3.5 to <4	45

Divide subtotal by number of items in strategy completed.

Consumer response has been tepid. The problem is that nothing tastes quite as good as fat. *Consumer Reports* tested a variety of nonfat pound cakes, frozen dairy desserts and yogurts and found that only the cakes and a few yogurts were palatable. In another survey, the magazine looked at reduced-fat versions of American cheese, Italian dressing, mayonnaise and oatmeal-raisin cookies. Only one nonfat cookie survived the test unscathed—and *(continued on page 112)*

Your Mother's Hearty Diet

Shocking as many of the items in this sample menu may look to an enlightened eater of the 1990s, this is the way Americans ate for decades—and truth be told, it's the way many of us eat now. Look at the total calories in the three menus: There are almost 350 more in this seemingly fat-laden diet than in "Your Modern Fake-Food Diet" on page 110 with its sugar substitutes and technology-created foods, and almost 650 more than in "The Commonsense, All-You-Need Diet" we recommend on page 100.

Nutritionists are beginning to revive the old idea that total calorie count is important, not just the components of a day's menu. Note the arguments for and against this old-fashioned way of eating, but remember that there's a reason people still eat this way. The food tastes good and makes you feel full.

Eggs. Eggs nearly disappeared from the diets of health-conscious Americans during the 1980s and early 1990s. But despite the fat and cholesterol in the yolks, eggs are still the "gold standard" of a perfect protein, meaning one in which the component amino acids are in an ideal balance that the human body can absorb. The American Heart Association has upped its recommended weekly egg allowance from three to four. So don't give them up entirely.

Cheese. Cheddar cheese, like all milk products, is a fine source of calcium, but unlike some other milk products, it's very high in fat. Don't write it off, though. Many people who are lactose-intolerant can digest aged Cheddar cheese.

Saltines. Salt isn't quite the enemy it was thought to be in the 1960s. The salt in a few saltines certainly won't kill you. It's the hydrogenated fat you should try to avoid. And that isn't hard to do; most manufacturers make low-fat (and low-salt) versions of our favorite crackers.

Whole milk. The calcium and protein in milk are invaluable, especially for women, who should consume several glasses of milk or cups of yogurt a day. But there isn't much of an excuse for whole milk in anyone's diet—unless it's a tablespoonful or so in coffee. A cup of whole milk has 8 grams of fat. Stick to 1 percent if you want some flavor and only 2.5 grams of fat.

Sirloin steak. It's hard to defend beef these days. Most cuts are high in cholesterol and saturated fat, and there are plenty of other sources of protein that have a lot less fat. Still, red meat offers substantial amounts of easily absorbed iron, copper and zinc, and lean cuts can be fit into a low-fat diet.

Breakfast
6 ounces freshly squeezed orange juice
2 eggs, scrambled
2 slices bacon
2 slices whole-wheat toast
2 teaspoons butter

Snack
4 saltines
1 ounce Cheddar cheese
1 apple

Lunch
Chicken salad sandwich made with ½ cup chicken salad on whole-wheat bread
8 ounces whole milk
1 orange

Snack
1 thick chocolate milk shake

Dinner
4 ounces broiled sirloin steak
Baked potato with 2 tablespoons sour cream
1 cup cooked green beans
1 tomato, sliced
8 ounces whole milk
1 slice apple pie

Totals: 2,784 calories, 117 grams fat (37 percent of calories), 46 percent of calories from carbohydrates, 18 percent of calories from protein, 706 milligrams cholesterol, 34 grams fiber, 3,196 milligrams sodium, 114 grams sugar.

Your Modern Fake-Food Diet

In the 1960s, everyone knew that a piece of raspberry crumb cake tasted better than a raspberry Pop-Tart. But who had the time to make crumb cake? Then the clever food manufacturers put vitamins and minerals into—and took fat out of—their packaged goods, making engineered foods not just convenient alternatives to cooking from scratch but seemingly healthier substitutes for the originals.

Unfortunately, what appeared to be nutrition nirvana turned out to be something much more complicated. When fat is removed from your crumb cake, it is usually replaced by something else that is seldom nutritious. In other words, you may be saved from whatever bad things fat does for you, but you may be replacing them with something equally bad.

SnackWell's cookies and Weight Watchers cheesecake. Remember, low-fat doesn't necessarily mean low-calorie. So check the serving size to see exactly how many calories— and how much food—are in one serving. If there are 60 calories in one cookie and you're eating five of those guys, your calorie savings are out the window. The problem is, manufacturers replace some of the lost fat with sugar. If it's dessert, chances are it's fattening.

Fruit Roll-Ups. These were invented for kids who can't stand the idea of putting real fruit into their mouths. But the gooey, sugary stuff, which sticks like glue to their teeth, will give them cavities. You, too. So go for the fiber and vitamins in real fruit, which will better satisfy your hunger anyway.

Light potato chips. It's nice to reduce the oil content of these grease delivery systems, but be sure the oil is a nonhydrogenated vegetable oil, such as canola. Only with the changes in labeling laws does light actually mean significant savings in calories, fat or, in the case of potato chips, sodium. (Continue to beware of light oils, which have just the flavor removed, not the calories.)

Breakfast
6 ounces orange juice
1 Pop-Tart
8 ounces 1 percent low-fat milk

Snack
1 slice cinnamon swirl coffee cake
1 12-ounce diet cola

Lunch
Bologna sandwich made with 3 slices Oscar Mayer light bologna, 1 slice processed American cheese and 2 teaspoons mayonnaise on white bread
1 12-ounce diet soda
3 SnackWell's devil's food cookie cake

Snack
Fruit Roll-Up
2 ounces light potato chips
1 12-ounce diet cola

Dinner
5 ounces breaded chicken cutlet
2 ounces frozen french fries
3 tablespoons ketchup

Snack
Salad: iceberg lettuce with 2 tablespoons low-calorie French dressing
1 slice Weight Watchers cheesecake
8 ounces diet iced tea

Totals: 2,436 calories, 100 grams fat (37 percent of calories), 50 percent of calories from carbohydrates, 14 percent of calories from protein, 224 milligrams cholesterol, 8 grams fiber, 4,162 milligrams sodium, 209 grams sugar.

it had nearly as many calories as the full-fat version.

Better flavor could come with time. For now, the question is: Are low-fat foods and fat replacements helping people eat better and lose weight?

In a study by Barbara J. Rolls, Ph.D., a researcher at the Johns Hopkins University School of Medicine in Baltimore, normal-weight subjects who, without knowing it, ate a low-fat breakfast (11 grams of fat) made with the fat replacement Olestra tended to compensate by eating more calories, but not more fat, later in the day.

Food Heroes and Villains

In theory, then, fat substitutes could help, but they haven't been around long enough for scientists to fairly judge their effects. Artificial sweeteners have. First, there was saccharin, the sweetener that unleashed a tidal wave of diet sodas in the early 1960s. Then came aspartame, the generic name for NutraSweet, which was approved by the Food and Drug Administration in 1981 and now appears in more than 4,000 foods and beverages. Although sales of diet sodas have flattened out in the past couple of years, the end is not in sight for artificial sweeteners. Sucralose, now awaiting the approval of the Food and Drug Administration, retains its sweetness longer than aspartame, which means it could be used in fruit juices, which have a longer shelf life than sodas. Also, unlike aspartame, you can cook with it, which opens up a whole new world of applications.

Yet the net effect of artificial sweeteners in reducing calorie intake appears to be nil, perhaps because many people use diet sodas as a kind of rain check that allows them to go on calorie splurges when dessert time rolls around. "Sugar substitutes were marketed in the 1950s as a way to cut back on sugar, but the use of sugar has gone up, as has the use of sweeteners," says Marion Franz, R.D., director of publications and nutrition at the International Diabetes Center in Minneapolis. In other words, Americans tend to want it both ways, to believe that there really is such a thing as a free (nonfat) lunch—a big one at that. Nutritionists have picked up on this, and portion size now looms as the dietary villain of the mid-1990s. The U.S. Department of Agriculture is publishing a Healthy Eating Index, emphasizing portion size, to help people know if they are following the government's Food Guide Pyramid.

THE NET EFFECT OF ARTIFICIAL SWEETENERS IN REDUCING CALORIE INTAKE APPEARS TO BE NIL.

"This is emblematic of the way Americans look at food," says Michelle Stacey, author of *Consumed: Why Americans Love, Hate and Fear Food*. "We want a single answer. It's like serial monogamy. If we say fat is the problem, we can say that everything else is okay, including all of the wonderful things that technology is coming up with, which is also very American. As a result, we're eating a lot more of these things, because they're less satisfying."

—*William Grimes with Corby Kummer*

Maximize Your Body's Fat-Burning Power

For any diet to work, it has to match your body's metabolic cycles. Here's a diet plan that does just that, keeping calorie burning high and fat storage low.

Once upon a time, dieting meant simply cutting calories. Eat less, weigh less. It seemed to make sense. Why, then, did it so often fail? Because, we now know, this dieting strategy is like swimming up the Colorado River. You might make some progress, but ultimately, you're no match for nature.

For a diet strategy to succeed, it has to acknowledge the body's natural metabolic currents and flow with them. Now, finally, here's one that does. By following this simple formula, you'll maximize your body's natural fat-burning potential and peel pounds permanently. Specifically, the diet plan calls for:

- Eating four daily meals—breakfast, lunch, a substantial afternoon snack and dinner, all approximately the same size
- Curbing fat intake while maintaining a moderate (not too low!) calorie intake
- Focusing on naturally low-fat, high-fiber foods such as vegetables, whole grains and legumes

- Keeping a watchful eye on refined and processed foods that are calorie-dense and fiber-depleted

Of course, it's vital to add to any eating plan a heaping serving of exercise. Exercise activates weight loss; it revs your metabolism so that you can eat enough calories to stay healthy.

Meal Planning

Spreading your daily calories over four meals is an effective way to speed the metabolism, minimize fat storage and dampen the appetite. Scientists have observed that missing meals, especially early in the day, is hazardous to the waistline. "Skipping breakfast and eating a moderate lunch and a huge dinner is the most common pattern for people with weight problems," notes James Kenney, R.D., Ph.D., a nutrition research specialist at the Pritikin Longevity Center in Santa Monica, California. Bypassing breakfast or lunch can leave you starving for dinner, resulting in overeating, and can slow metabolism.

> **P**EOPLE WHO EAT **BREAKFAST BURN MORE CALORIES THAN BREAKFAST SKIPPERS.**

"We found that people who skip breakfast or breakfast and lunch burn about 5 percent fewer calories than people who are eating three meals or more a day," says obesity expert C. Wayne Callaway, M.D., associate clinical professor of medicine at George Washington University in Washington, D.C. This pattern also affects production of the hormone insulin, which encourages fat production and storage, says Dr. Kenney. Large meals cause the body to release more insulin. The time of day seems to make a difference, too. "In the evening, the body responds better to insulin," says Dr. Kenney. "That means it stores fat more efficiently at dinnertime."

The alternative—eating smaller, more frequent meals—not only reduces insulin but boosts metabolism, burning more calories as well.

So a better plan would be to eat about 25 percent of your daily calories at breakfast and another 25 percent at lunch. Add a substantial afternoon snack, also containing about 20 to 25 percent of your daily calories. (Research shows that small snacks—less than 10 percent of daily calories—don't raise the metabolic rate significantly.) Then prepare a moderate dinner with about the same number of calories as your earlier meals. If you need an after-dinner snack, make it light and low-fat. If you've eaten well earlier in the day, you won't be so ravenously hungry for late-night munchies.

Calorie Considerations

In determining your daily intake, it's important to keep your eye on two different horizons: fat and calories. While fat reduction is the most important priority for good health and weight loss, you don't want calories to fall too low or climb too high.

A good rule of thumb for women trying to lose extra weight is to eat 10 calories for every pound of your current weight; men's limit is about 12 calories. You can afford 2 or 3 additional calories per pound if you exercise for at least 30 minutes three times a week. This pace would result in shedding a half-pound to one pound a week, which studies show is the rate of weight loss that's most likely to be permanent and to prevent the loss of valuable fat-burning muscle.

As for fat, most experts suggest about 20 to 25 percent of calories from fat. For best results, we recommend that

Best Ideas for Dieters' Danger Zones

At the supermarket. Never, ever shop on an empty stomach.

At mealtime. Preplan. "If you plan a healthy salad, you're more likely to follow through," says Georgia Kostas, R.D., director of nutrition at the Cooper Clinic in Dallas and author of *Balancing Act Nutrition and Weight Guide.* "If you don't make plans, a hamburger will sound great."

After a meal. Pop a sugar-free mint or butterscotch candy into your mouth; resisting dessert will be easier.

At a restaurant. Order extra side dishes of rice and steamed vegetables. Eat more of those, less of the meat.

At a buffet party. After a few hors d'oeuvres, sneak off to the bathroom to brush your teeth. You'll be less likely to eat more Swedish meatballs if they're going to taste like spearmint.

At the office. Visit the watercooler often or keep a carafe of water at your desk. Eight glasses of water a day keeps you more satisfied and prevents overeating. A lot of people overeat from thirst, mistaking it for hunger, notes Kostas.

After dinner. Clean up the kitchen, turn off the lights and shut down the kitchen for the night, so you won't keep going back for snacks, Kostas suggests.

In front of the television. Put a Thermos of ice water or hot tea on your television table. Or lay out a preplanned healthy snack, such as a measured amount of low-fat microwave popcorn.

On the weekend. Make firm plans to eat every four to six hours. "If you are running errands and don't eat, the tendency is to get overly hungry and use your free time in a mall to grab high-calorie snacks instead of healthier choices," notes Kostas.

calories from fat not exceed 20 percent of your daily calories, which is a ceiling of about 33 grams of fat for someone eating 1,500 calories a day, 40 grams for someone eating 1,800 calories and 51 grams for someone eating 2,300 calories.

If you're uncertain about how many fat grams or calories you're consuming, keep a food diary for a couple of days. Then use a fat and calorie counter to find your totals. A food diary is a winning technique. "Keeping records is consistently associated with long-term success in weight control," says Dr. Callaway.

On the other hand, if you just don't have the patience to count calories and fat grams, there is an easy rule that will usually point you in the right direction. Focus your eating on whole foods: whole grains, vegetables, legumes and fruits.

> **I**F YOU DON'T HAVE THE PATIENCE TO COUNT CALORIES, FOCUS ON WHOLE FOODS: GRAINS, VEGETABLES, LEGUMES AND FRUITS.

Choose an apple instead of apple juice, brown rice instead of white rice, a whole baked potato instead of french fries, a fresh apricot instead of an apricot Danish. The less-processed versions are likely to contain less sugar, less fat and more nutrients. And most important for weight watchers, whole foods tend to contain more fiber, which fills you up, so you feel more satisfied on fewer calories. Fiber also minimizes insulin response, so less fat is stored.

—Cathy Perlmutter with Michele Stanten

Optimum Nutrition for Serious Dieters

Cutting calories can shortchange you on nutrients. That's why dieters often take supplements. Here's what you need to know to select an appropriate multiple—and a few single-nutrient supplements you should consider.

Ever skip breakfast? Ever wish you had skipped lunch after you realized how unhealthy it was? You are not alone. Only one in eight of us, dieters included, eats even the minimum five fruits and veggies every day. No wonder surveys by the National Institutes of Health in Bethesda, Maryland, and the U.S. Department of Agriculture suggest many Americans routinely get less—often much less— than 100 percent of the Daily Values (DVs) for key vitamins and minerals.

Even careful eaters may be falling short. When dietitians at Utah State University in Logan tried to design balanced menus that met the government's dietary guidelines, they had trouble achieving all vitamin and mineral goals for adult women with less than 2,200 calories. That means anyone who usually consumes under 2,200 calories, which includes most women, many dieters and seniors, may fall below at least some DVs.

Slowly and silently, these shortfalls may undermine long-term health. "Let's say I eat too little magnesium, which most Americans do," says David McCarron, M.D., director of the Clinical Nutrition Research Unit at Oregon Health Sciences University in Portland. "That forces my cells to make trade-offs, none of which makes me sick right away but some of which may contribute to chronic illness years down the road, especially if I have an inherited weakness or two."

> **E**VEN DIETITIANS HAVE TROUBLE DESIGNING MENUS THAT MEET DIETARY GUIDELINES WITH CALORIE COUNTS OF LESS THAN **2,200.**

Hundreds of studies have linked diets high in essential nutrients to lower rates of disease, though only controlled tests of supplements versus placebos can prove that it's the vitamins and minerals that protect us. Nevertheless, some researchers now see chronic illnesses such as heart disease, high blood pressure, diabetes and cancer at least partially as deficiency diseases, the way we already think of rickets and scurvy.

The best solution to diet shortfalls? Eating the healthiest foods you can—lots of veggies, fruits, whole grains and low-fat dairy products. All of the experts we consulted suggest that it's the potent cocktail of vitamins, minerals, fiber and substances available only in foods—the phytochemicals, for instance—that best explains the protective power of a healthy diet.

Beyond that, most experts agree that closing some nutritional gaps with a balanced multivitamin/mineral supplement (multi for short) either can't hurt or just plain makes sense. "It's not a magic bullet, but it is a small, logical insurance policy, especially since there's no evidence of harm," says Harvard University epidemiologist Walter Willett, M.D.

Even many dietitians, surveys show, now take multis.

No research has linked multis with a longer life span. But preliminary evidence suggests—not surprisingly—that multis may increase our "health span," the years we're free from chronic illness. In a study among people over age 65, moderate use of multis cut in half the number of days of infection-related illness. Use of multis has been linked with fewer cataracts. And folic acid–containing multis helped decrease the number of serious nervous system defects in babies born in Hungary to mothers who took supplements.

What Your Multi Should Have

There's a multitude of multis out there. But many are incomplete, with important nutrients missing or too low, or too complete, with higher than warranted doses. So check labels. (You'll need good eyes or good glasses for this!) Your multi should include the following.

Vitamin A/beta-carotene. Aim for 100 percent of the DV for vitamin A (5,000 international units), some of which may come from beta-carotene, a vitamin A precursor. (The beta-carotene equivalent of 100 percent of the DV is three milligrams.) Diets rich in beta-carotene, an important antioxidant, have been linked with lower rates of lung, breast and many other cancers, heart disease, stroke and cataracts. But whether supplements of beta-carotene well above DV range are beneficial is controversial and is awaiting the results of ongoing studies. On the plus side, preliminary results from Harvard University's famous Physicians Health Study show that doctors with heart disease who took 50 milligrams of beta-carotene every other day for

SURVEYS SHOW THAT MANY DIETITIANS NOW TAKE MULTIS.

six years had half as many strokes, fatal heart attacks and angioplasties as doctors who took placebos.

Niacin. Aim for 100 percent of the DV (20 milligrams). Niacin in high doses (1,000 milligrams plus) is useful for some heart patients because it raises "good" HDL cholesterol and lowers triglycerides. But because of the possibility of serious side effects—including liver damage, especially from slow-release niacin—these super-high doses must be taken only under a doctor's supervision.

Folic acid. Aim for 100 percent of the DV (listed on labels either as 400 micrograms or 0.4 milligram). Surveys show many Americans, and especially women, are falling far short of this level. Getting enough of this emerging superstar vitamin is the number one reason to take a multivitamin/mineral supplement, says Meir Stampfer, M.D., of the Harvard School of Public Health. The U.S. Public Health Service urges all women of childbearing age to get 400 micrograms of folic acid daily to help prevent serious brain and spinal cord defects in babies.

Beyond this, diets low in folic acid are associated with high blood levels of homocysteine, a newly studied substance with a strong connection to heart disease. Diets high in folic acid appear linked with lower risk of cervical and colon cancer.

Vitamin B_6. Aim for 100 percent of the DV (2 milligrams). American diets are low in vitamin B_6 (and for some women, long-term use of oral contraceptives appears to increase B_6 needs). Low B_6 intakes are linked with high homocysteine levels, greater heart attack risk and poor functioning of the immune system in older people. *Caution:* Doses of 500 milligrams or more a day have been associated with nerve damage.

Vitamin B_{12}. Aim for 100 percent of the DV (six micrograms). Here's yet another B vitamin linked with higher levels of homocysteine and heart disease in those who consume or absorb the least. Lack of enough B_{12} in the elderly is also associated with memory loss and disorientation, symptoms that can mimic Alzheimer's disease. Since older people may have trouble absorbing B_{12}, any suspected deficiencies in this age group should be treated by a physician. Strict vegetarians may especially need to supplement, because B_{12} is found almost exclusively in animal products.

IT'S DIFFICULT TO GET EVEN THE MINIMUM **50** MICROGRAMS OF CHROMIUM ON LESS THAN **3,000** CALORIES A DAY.

Vitamin D. Aim for 100 percent of the DV (400 international units). You need enough vitamin D to make it possible to absorb the calcium you eat, though you don't have to consume the two nutrients at the same time. Good sources of vitamin D are sunshine on the skin and vitamin D–fortified milk. For those who can't achieve adequate vitamin D intakes through diet, supplements may be the simplest solution. Don't supplement more than 400 international units without your doctor's supervision; high levels can be toxic.

Chromium. Aim for 50 to 200 micrograms, a safe range set by the National Research Council in Washington, D.C. Supplements may be the only way for most of us to get enough chromium. Studies by U.S. Department of Agriculture vitamin and mineral specialist Richard Anderson, Ph.D., demonstrate that it's difficult to get even the minimum 50 micrograms of chromium on less than 3,000 calories a day. Chromium forms part of a substance called glucose tolerance factor, which helps our cells absorb the blood sugar we convert to energy. Very preliminary research indicates that chromium supplements may improve glucose handling in people with diabetes and shrink elevated cholesterol levels. (Research showing that chromium may promote weight loss and develop muscle mass is conflicting at this time.)

Copper. Aim for 100 percent of the DV (two milligrams). Copper acts as part of an important antioxidant enzyme system that seems to play a role in heart health. According to Dr. Anderson, however, most Americans' diets supply less than half of the copper we need. Above all, make sure any multi that has 100 percent of the DV for zinc also has 100 percent of the DV for copper; some don't. Elevating zinc intake without taking in enough copper can lead to copper deficiency.

> **M**OST **A**MERICANS' **DIETS** **SUPPLY LESS THAN HALF OF** **THE COPPER WE NEED.**

Iron. Premenopausal women should aim for 100 percent of the DV (18 milligrams); adult men and postmenopausal women should aim for 0 to 50 percent of the DV (0 to 9 milligrams). Women having periods, especially those with heavy bleeding and those who exercise, may well need supplements to ensure that they get enough iron, though they should not take more than 18 milligrams unless diagnosed with iron-deficiency anemia. (In that case, iron supplementation will be directed by your physician.) In men and postmenopausal women, levels of body iron stores rise with age. High levels of iron have been associated with increased risk of heart attack in some studies, though other studies have found no link.

Magnesium. Aim for at least 25 percent of the DV (100 milligrams), the most you're likely to find in a single-dose supplement. (Otherwise, the capsule would be too big to swallow.) Diets low in magnesium have been linked with high blood pressure, and the National Institutes of Health now recommends adequate magnesium intake as one way to keep blood pressure normal. Small studies have shown that magnesium supplements can help reduce elevated blood pressure and may make insulin work better in some people who have diabetes.

Surveys show that most Americans' diets are low in magnesium, with men getting an average of 329 milligrams, and women, 207 milligrams. An extra 100 milligrams in your multi may be enough to put you in pretty good shape, especially if you're eating magnesium-rich seeds, nuts, legumes and whole grains. But to be certain, you might want to consider adding magnesium as a single supplement at no more than 400 milligrams. (Excess magnesium can lead to diarrhea. Those with abnormal kidney function should not supplement magnesium without a doctor's supervision.)

Selenium. Aim for 70 to 100 micrograms, a safe range suggested by our experts. Selenium plays a role in glutathione peroxidase, a powerful antioxidant enzyme. In China, selenium supplements (combined with supplements of beta-carotene and vitamin E) reduced the risk of dying from cancer among a large population deficient in these nutrients. In Italy, deaths from heart disease rose dramatically among residents of a village whose public water supply was changed from wells high in selenium to water with a lower selenium content. Stay in the recommended safe range; selenium is toxic at higher intakes, particularly over one milligram a day.

Zinc. Aim for 100 percent of the DV (15 milligrams). Zinc is known to be necessary for proper wound healing and a strong immune system. Yet surveys show it may be the mineral most lacking in U.S. diets. Zinc supplements improved signs of immune function in two studies among elderly people at risk for zinc deficiency. Paradoxically,

Supplement-Shopper's Checklist

Multivitamin/mineral supplement. Make sure your multivitamin/mineral formula provides all of the following:

- 100 percent of the Daily Values (DVs) for vitamin A/beta-carotene, niacin, vitamin B_6, folic acid, vitamin B_{12}, vitamin D, copper and zinc (other nutrients may also be present at up to 100 percent of the DVs)
- Chromium: 50 to 200 micrograms
- Selenium: 70 to 100 micrograms
- Iron: Men and postmenopausal women, 0 to 50 percent of the DV (0 to 9 milligrams); premenopausal women, 100 percent of the DV (18 milligrams)
- Magnesium: 25 percent of the DV (100 milligrams); accept no less in a single-dose multi

Calcium supplement. 500 to 1,000 milligrams. (Usually, this requires more than one tablet.)
Vitamin C supplement. 100 to 500 milligrams.
Vitamin E supplement. 100 to 400 international units.

supplementing with too much zinc—25 milligrams a day in one study—may backfire and weaken the immune system.

Three Sensible Singles

Beyond a basic multi, we think there's persuasive reason to add single supplements of calcium, vitamin C and vitamin E to your program. Here's why.

Calcium. If you're a woman, chances are strong you need a separate calcium supplement, because no single-dose multi that we've seen contains 100 percent of the DV (1,000 milligrams). Most multis have 200 milligrams or less.

It's clear from many studies that adequate calcium lowers the risk of osteoporosis, the bone-thinning disease that affects half of all women over age 50. You would have to drink more than three cups of milk a day to get 1,000 milligrams of calcium.

Your goal: Women ages 25 to 50 and men ages 25 to 65—1,000 milligrams; women and men under 25—1,200 to 1,500 milligrams; women over 50 and men over 65—1,500 milligrams. To determine how much calcium you need to supplement, find your goal. Then subtract the amount of calcium in your multi and 300 milligrams for each serving of milk, yogurt, cheese and calcium-fortified orange juice you normally eat. Many women need 500 to 1,000 milligrams of supplemental calcium a day.

Vitamin C. There's evidence that intake of this antioxidant vitamin at levels above the DV (60 milligrams) has added protective effects. During a large ten-year government study, men consuming an average of 300 milligrams of vitamin C per day, partly from supplements, had almost half of the deaths from heart disease of men taking in less than 50 milligrams a day. Research shows that higher vitamin C intake is associated with higher HDL and lower total and "bad" LDL cholesterol levels.

Intake of high–vitamin C foods has been linked with protection against cancers of the digestive tract, cervix, rectum, breast and lung.

Your goal: 100 to 500 milligrams of vitamin C daily. This amount is safe; some people get diarrhea at intakes of 1,000 milligrams or more.

Vitamin E. Here's another key antioxidant vitamin that we think it makes sense to take at levels above the DV (30 international units). Two large observational studies among nurses and male health professionals found that those who took at least 100 international units of vitamin E a day in supplement form for at least two years had a risk of heart disease approximately 40 percent lower than those who consumed about 10 international units a day through diet alone.

Higher levels of vitamin E appear to boost signs of immune function in the elderly, according to research. Preliminary evidence suggests that supplements of vitamin E may reduce the risk of cataracts and some cancers and may have some positive effects for people with diabetes.

To get vitamin E at levels that appear to be protective, you must supplement.

Your goal: 100 to 400 international units appears to be safe. But because a study in Finland showed a slightly increased risk of stroke due to hemorrhage in people taking 50 international units of vitamin E daily, you should check with your doctor before starting vitamin E supplements if you are on blood-thinning medicine, take aspirin regularly or have a history of bleeding disorders, including ulcers.

—Holly McCord, R.D.

Part V

Turning the Tide on Temptation

Why You Gotta Have It— And How to Get around It

Cravings aren't just psychological. They have strong physiological components that can make some foods practically addictive. Here's how to pick food choices that satisfy cravings without piling on pounds.

Ninety-seven percent of young women and 68 percent of young men give in to food cravings at least now and then. What's behind the urge to indulge? Many things, actually. Cravings can be the result of childhood food associations, memories, cultural beliefs and traditions or other powerful emotional cues. Some cravings may be mere habits; if a sweet midafternoon snack makes you feel good, you're likely to have it again and again. The body's chemistry also influences when and what you eat, and what you eat both directly and indirectly affects how you feel.

Many neurotransmitters—the brain chemicals that connect nerve endings and regulate how we think, feel and behave—become more or less active depending on dietary intake. Either overconsuming or dramatically restricting a particular food, such as fat or carbohydrates, may trigger imbalances in neuro-transmitters that then affect behavior. That's why it is so important to develop a plan that both controls the urge to overload on non-nutritious treats and keeps the brain's chemistry in balance.

But cravings often seem impossible to resist. Just about every aspect of life, from chemicals produced in the brain, intestinal tract and other organs to the aroma of just-baked cinnamon rolls, triggers the appetite. Yet succumbing to temptation not only expands our waistlines but also tends to make us feel weak and vulnerable. Women in particular often feel guilty or angry with themselves when they give in. Fortunately, there are ways to keep from overindulging without feeling utterly deprived. The following are three of the most common food cravings, plus tips on how to conquer them.

Cranky without Carbohydrates?

Most of us occasionally find it hard to just say no to a sweet treat or another carbohydrate-laden snack. But some people battle cravings daily and can't seem to resist these foods. Seemingly levelheaded people can become anxious or irritable if they don't have their morning doughnuts or afternoon sodas. This is not a sign of lack of willpower, however; research is uncovering a far more complex and deep-seated cause of those irresistible urges.

RESEARCH IS UNCOVERING A FAR MORE COMPLEX AND DEEP-SEATED CAUSE OF THOSE IRRESISTIBLE URGES.

Some people crave carbohydrates, postulates Richard J. Wurtman, M.D., professor of brain and cognitive sciences at the Massachusetts Institute of Technology in Cambridge, because they have low levels of serotonin, the neurotransmitter that regulates sleep, reduces pain and appetite, calms you down and influences your mood. Here's how it works: Eating a carbohydrate-rich meal stimulates the release of insulin, which in turn lowers blood levels of all amino acids except tryptophan. Tryptophan levels in the brain rise, and tryptophan is then converted to serotonin. And so to relieve mental fatigue, hunger, depression and stress thought to be brought on by their low serotonin levels, cravers turn to cookies, cakes, pastas and breads. They eventually become conditioned to crave carbohydrate-loaded foods whenever they are tired, depressed or anxious.

> THE MERE TASTE OF SUGAR ON THE TONGUE PRODUCES AN IMMEDIATE RUSH OF MORPHINELIKE ENDORPHINS.

Carbohydrate cravings may also be fueled by the desire and need for pleasurable sensations. For newborns, the mere taste of sugar on the tongue produces an immediate rush of endorphins, the morphinelike chemicals in the brain that may produce euphoric or relaxing responses. Based on her studies of infants, Barbara Smith, Ph.D., assistant adjunct professor of psychology at the Johns Hopkins University in Baltimore, suggests sugar activates the endorphins that ease stress and discomfort. "The sweet taste (of sugar) might stimulate the release of these endorphins and result in a calming effect," she says.

If you are a carbohydrate craver, here are a few important considerations when designing an eating plan.

Eat small meals and snacks throughout the day. And be sure they include some complex carbohydrates, such as whole-grain breads, starchy vegetables and legumes. These nutrient-packed foods satisfy serotonin needs without aggravating brain chemicals or blood sugar.

Always eat breakfast. And include at least one serving

of grains and one serving of fruit in the meal to keep your-self full and satisfied. Skipping breakfast may only increase cravings later in the morning.

Exercise. People who exercise regularly maintain their weight and are less prone to cravings, because exercise regulates blood sugar levels. Working out is also an alter-native to sugary foods for getting the pleasurable endor-phin rush and reducing stress.

Plan your snacks. If you love sweets, allow a certain number of calories for a small snack, but make it low in fat—nonfat frozen yogurt, fruit ices, vanilla wafers or fig bars. Abstinence tends to lead to binge eating.

Drink plenty of water. A desire for sweets in the evening could actually be a signal that the body needs fluids. Some people report that their cravings for ice cream subside within a few minutes of drinking one or two glasses of water.

Subduing the "Fat Tooth"

Although many people assume they crave sweets, in re-ality they may be searching for fat. Based on his own re-search, Adam Drewnowski, Ph.D., director of the human nutrition program at the University of Michigan in Ann Arbor, disagrees with the theory that people crave carbohy-drates alone. His studies show that it is a desire for fat—or, more specifically, for sweet-ened fat—that leads people to indulge in chocolate, ice cream and cookies. "These so-called carbohydrate-rich foods derive as many, if not more, of their calories from fat as from sugar," says Dr. Drewnowski. "The sugar just makes the fat taste better."

> **T**HE CRAVING FOR FAT IS MOSTLY UNCONSCIOUS.

Dr. Drewnowski's studies of food preferences, using

Craving Busters

In addition to finding acceptable substitutes for tempting snacks, try these methods the next time a craving threatens to overcome you.

Think before you nibble. Ask yourself: "Am I really hungry? Is this food what I really want to eat?" If the answer is yes to both questions, then have just a small helping. If the answer is no, then identify what you really want—a glass of water or a breath of fresh air.

Pinpoint your true desire. Are you yearning for something sweet? Crunchy? Chewy? Once you know exactly what you want, find a low-fat food that will satisfy that craving.

Break the habit. Take a long walk or call a friend during the time of day you would normally be heading for the refrigerator.

Ride the crave wave. A craving is similar to a wave that builds, then breaks on the beach, suggests G. Alan Marlatt, Ph.D., professor of psychology at the University of Washington in Seattle. Visualize yourself riding the rising urge like a wave until it crests and then subsides.

Get the details. Recording when, what and how much you eat and how you feel before and after eating can pinpoint the internal signals that are causing the cravings.

Eat small, eat slowly. Focus on the food. Take small bites and chew them slowly. This way, you'll be likely to eat less and still be satisfied.

Get support. Tailor your home and work environments to support healthful eating. Eliminate tempting foods from your environment, keep healthy snacks on hand and encourage support from friends and family.

varying amounts of sugar and fat, show that people are least likely to choose high-sugar, low-fat foods, such as jelly beans and Popsicles, and more likely to choose sweet foods that are also creamy, such as ice cream. The craving for fat is mostly unconscious. Because dietary fat is largely responsible for the texture, flavor and odor of a food, they make foods tantalizing.

Instead of fighting your fat craving, work with it, using these suggestions.

Slowly reduce your intake of dietary fat. If your body is accustomed to a large serving of something sweet and fat-filled late at night, reduce the serving size and gradually substitute more nutritious foods.

Focus on fiber. Fruits, vegetables, whole grains and legumes are fiber-packed foods that are filling without being fattening. At every meal and snack, include at least one serving each of fresh fruits and vegetables, whole-grain breads and cereals, and legumes such as kidney beans, chick-peas and black beans.

Avoid fatty meals and snacks at midday. They may set you up for more fat cravings at night. Try fresh fruits and vegetables, pretzels or a bagel with nonfat cream cheese.

Use low-fat or nonfat plain or vanilla yogurt. It can stand in for whipped cream, sour cream or ice cream as a topping for fruit or in a blender shake.

Look for low-fat, reduced-calorie versions of traditional packaged desserts and snacks. But remember that even these treats should be eaten in moderation because they are often high in sugar.

Spice it up. For the extra flavor you may be craving, add cinnamon, nutmeg or vanilla extract to nonfat yogurt, low-fat cereal or angel food cake.

Thinnest, Richest Chocolate Treats!

Sometimes our lips demand chocolate. Serious chocolate. But our hearts (and hips!) fare better without the troublesome calories and fat in standard chocolate yummies. The answer? Four indulgences that deliver rich chocolate satisfaction with modest fat and calorie price tags. Almost all of these products come packaged in individual servings. That gives you a built-in finish line!

	Fat (g.)	Calories
Dannon Light chocolate frozen yogurt (1 cup)	0	160
Yoplait low-fat chocolate mousse frozen yogurt bar	1	30
Whitney's low-fat chocolate cappucino supreme yogurt	2	200
Quaker Chewy low-fat chocolate chunk granola bar	2	110
Milky Way low-fat milk shake	3	220

Help for Chocoholics

Chocolate is America's favorite dessert flavor. In one year, we spent more than $6 billion on the heavenly stuff.

Cravings for sweets and chocolate are particularly related to depression. "It's no wonder people turn to chocolate when depressed or stressed," says Dr. Drewnowski. "Chocolate is a combination of sugar, fat and other compounds (including caffeine and phenylethylamine) that might stimulate the release of endorphins in the brain, which results in an analgesic effect." The endorphins produce such a powerful pleasure sensation that anything that stimulates their production is likely to be habit-forming.

A person craves carbohydrates such as chocolate because they stimulate the release of serotonin, which produces a feeling of calm, speculates Judith Wurtman, Ph.D., professor of brain and cognitive sciences at the Massachusetts Institute of Technology. Chocolate also contains theobromine and caffeine, compounds that provide a mental lift.

> **M**ORE THAN ANY OTHER CRAVING, CHOCOLATE URGES ARE NOT LIKELY TO JUST GO AWAY.

No one knows precisely why we love chocolate, but few will deny the cravings are real. More than any other craving, chocolate urges are not likely to just go away. So the best tactic is to include a small chocolate snack in your eating plan but give it a low-fat face-lift. Here are a few ideas for treats that fit these guidelines.

Look for chocolate-flavored syrups with one gram or less of fat. Spoon them over nonfat vanilla yogurt, fresh strawberries and orange slices, or use them as dips for frozen grapes and bananas.

Eat chocolate as a postmeal dessert rather than as a snack. When you already have food in your stomach, you'll be less likely to overindulge.

Buy chocolate in small quantities. That is, buy one or two chocolate kisses or miniature candy bars instead of a five-pound box.

—Elizabeth Somer, R.D.

Food Cravings:
When to Give In

Can you bypass bingeing by letting yourself have the treats you crave? A new no-denial theory says yes and shows you how to still stay in control.

Does the thought of french fries fill you with desire? Now many nutrition experts—yes, the ones who normally tell us what not to eat—are saying it's okay to have them. They do add "in moderation," of course. But their views reflect a new theory about food cravings that takes pleasure (yours) into consideration.

It's a good thing, too, because surveys show that people have cravings regularly. When the lust comes on, chances are you feel at war with your body. "If we try to ignore cravings, they often backfire, and we end up bingeing," says Robin Kanarek, Ph.D., professor of psychology and nutrition at Tufts University in Medford, Massachusetts.

Dr. Kanarek calls this abstinence violation, or the what-the-hell effect. The scenario: After resisting a cookie for hours (or days), you give in and eat one. Then since you've blown your diet, you finish off the package. Today's alternative scenario: When you crave a cookie, have one—just one—and don't obsess about it.

Why You Gotta Have It

This welcome advice is backed by research showing that cravings are more than idle desires; they could be conveying important information about your mind or body. Some experts believe cravings are the body's way of signaling a lack of certain nutrients. Others say that cravings represent psychological needs and that we get a mental boost from eating certain foods.

For example, Adam Drewnoski, Ph.D., director of the human nutrition program at the University of Michigan in Ann Arbor, has found that chocolate and other fatty foods cause the body to release mood-elevating endorphins. In fact, mood is the most common denominator behind cravings, reports Andrew Hill, Ph.D., senior lecturer at Leeds University in

> CRAVINGS ARE MORE THAN IDLE DESIRES; THEY COULD BE CONVEYING IMPORTANT INFORMATION ABOUT YOUR MIND OR BODY.

England. People tend to suffer food lust when they're angry, lonely, bored, upset or irritable—and they feel better after yielding to their yearnings. (The exception appears to be women with eating disorders, who often feel depressed after giving in.) Of course, if you're chronically upset, the fix isn't in your refrigerator. You need to get to the root of the problem. ·

As long as you don't overeat or want chocolate every few hours, it's okay to give in. But don't tempt yourself if you aren't sure you can handle it. If you can't stop at one scoop of ice cream, don't keep a gallon in the house, says

Have Your Cake and Eat It, Too

An apple won't cut it when you really want ice cream. If you're watching your weight, choose low-fat foods that resemble those your crave.

If You Crave	Give In to
Cake	Angel food cake—it's low in calories and fat (avoid nonfat cakes, which tend to have a lot of sugar)
Candy	Hard candies; jelly beans; licorice; fresh berries, watermelon, grapes, mango or kiwifruit
Chips	Reduced-fat or nonfat potato chips; baked corn tortilla chips; pretzels; air-popped popcorn; rice cakes
Chocolate	Dietetic hot chocolate; chocolate sugar-free pudding; nonfat chocolate ice cream or frozen yogurt; Fudgsicles
Cookies	Graham and animal crackers (nonfat cookies are an okay second choice but can be high in calories)
Fast food	A plain burger, or a cheeseburger you make yourself with low-fat cheese
French fries	Low-fat "fries" you make yourself by tossing potato slices in ½ teaspoon olive oil, sprinkling them with paprika and baking at 400° until crisp (avoid frozen fries—they're precooked in oil)
Ice cream	Low-fat or nonfat frozen yogurt; sorbet; ices; frozen-fruit pops
Pizza	Pizza with half of the usual amount of cheese and veggies instead of meats, or a low-fat frozen pizza

Linda Crawford, an eating behavior counselor at Green Mountain at Fox Run, a weight management center in Ludlow, Vermont. She advises those with frequent cravings to distract themselves for ten minutes. Then if you still want candy, eat it and forget it. Says Crawford, "People who learn not to make a big deal out of cravings tend not to have weight problems."

—Holland Sweet

Outsmart Your Appetite

These seven strategies will help you beguile your taste buds into loving low-fat foods. Honest.

Diet soda aficionados like me are privy to a powerful yet little-known truth: We can train our taste buds to prefer low-calorie foods and drinks over the full-calorie originals. My fairly typical story provides a case in point.

I started drinking diet soda in college because I wanted to lose a few pounds. It was a real sacrifice; I hated the way it tasted. Then at some indefinable time closer to then than to now, I became partial to that distinctively tinny taste I once hated. And now I actually like the stuff so much that I drink it with french fries, with cookies and with ice cream (the ultimate caloric contradiction).

Researchers say the change in taste preference that I experienced can occur with foods as well as with drinks—and that there's a whole slew of new scientific evidence to prove as much. "The preference for high- or low-fat foods doesn't appear to be biological," explains Deborah J. Bowen, Ph.D., a psychologist at the Fred Hutchinson Cancer Research Center in Seattle, who is conducting a study of food preferences in women. "In fact, we think that the women in our study who dislike fat may be using some sort of coping mechanism to help them avoid high-fat foods."

What is this magical mechanism? Perhaps it's simply the knowledge that fat will pad their waistlines, so they tell themselves that don't like it, postulates Dr. Bowen. Or maybe it's because they anticipate that high-fat foods will upset their stomachs and make them feel uncomfortable. (High-fat foods often take a long time to digest and can cause indigestion in people who are unaccustomed to eating them.) Then again, it may be something else entirely.

For instance, a series of studies conducted at the Monell Chemical Senses Center in Philadelphia revealed that people who are deprived of the "mouth-feel" of fat (its thickness and creaminess) also come to favor low-fat products. In one of these experiments, 27 participants were divided into three groups and studied for six months. The first group was instructed to follow a low-fat diet, consuming just 20 percent of total calories from fat, and to cut out all sources of added fat (butter, margarine, mayonnaise, salad dressing, sour cream and the like—both the full-fat and the reduced-fat varieties). The second group was also told to eat a low-fat diet, but they were permitted to indulge in fat substitutes. The third group ate anything and everything they wanted.

> **P**EOPLE WHO ARE DEPRIVED OF THE "MOUTH-FEEL" OF FAT COME TO FAVOR LOW-FAT PRODUCTS.

The outcome? "The first group developed a heightened acceptance of low-fat foods over high-fat foods, while the second and third groups exhibited no change in their attitudes toward fat," says researcher Richard Mattes, R.D., Ph.D. "Our study indicates that the preference for fatty foods is dictated more by sensory exposure than by a metabolic cue. As a species, we simply develop a taste for the foods that are available." And these foods are, by and large, fatty ones.

The overriding weight-loss lesson in all of these studies is the same: The key to permanent weight loss is largely in the mind. Therefore, much as I came to savor diet soda and disfavor the full-calorie kind, you can learn to relish low-fat foods and loathe high-fat ones. All you have to do is train your brain and trick your taste buds. Following are seven ways to do just that.

Start slowly. "Changing your eating habits takes time," says Lorri Fishman, R.D., a spokesperson for the National Center for Nutrition and Dietetics of the American Dietetic Association in Chicago. "To reduce the fat in your diet, you must start gradually and be patient." In fact, studies show that it takes about three months to derail any habit—and for most Americans, fat is a habit. So treat it as such.

Here's how: Gradually reduce your consumption of high-fat items by fighting one fatty food at a time. If you regularly eat fried chicken three times a week, for instance, try to limit your consumption. Indulge only once a week, and when you do, make the oven-baked version that uses little, if any, oil. Or remove all of the crunchy coating and skin from the fried variety (the skin on poultry contains most of the fat). Next, reduce your consumption of ice cream, then butter, then chocolate. And continue in this manner until you have all of your fatty favorites under control.

At the same time, increase your consumption of fruits, grains and vegetables, and limit the amount of high-fat meat and dairy products you eat. For instance, if you typically eat one piece of fruit a day (say, a sliced banana on top of your morning cereal), add an apple or pear at lunch and an orange for an evening snack, instead of your usual cookies or cake. You'll lower your fat consumption in the long run, because you'll end up replacing high-fat snacks with low-fat pieces of fruit.

As for meat and dairy foods: Just limit the amount you eat to two to three servings (of each) per day, and substitute baked chicken or grilled fish for fattier red meat.

Defat high-fat recipes. Just because you're reducing dietary fat doesn't mean your favorite family recipes are off-limits. You simply have to be creative, fiddling with Grandma's Chicken Surprise to replace her high-fat surprises with healthful ingredients. Your efforts will allow you to enjoy the dishes you love without guilt.

Two tricks: Substitute lower-fat ingredients for fatty ones (a splash of citrus juice, wine or vinegar for oil; yogurt for mayonnaise; reduced-fat tofu or lean meat for fatty beef; evaporated skim milk for heavy cream), which will actually enhance the flavors of many dishes. And adjust both the type and the amount of fat a recipe calls for (you can typically reduce fat by one-third to one-half without affecting taste). For instance, try using ¼ cup of olive or canola oil in place of ⅓ cup of butter, which is high in artery-clogging saturated fat. This strategy may require some initial experimentation, but the reduced-fat results will be well worth your efforts.

Think big picture. Remember the women in Dr. Bowen's study who developed a distaste for fatty fare? They managed to embrace a healthful mind-set about food that affected their outlook on life in general. They told Dr. Bowen that they felt more vigorous and positive—in fact, they suffered fewer bouts of the blues—when they abstained from high-fat fare. And they relished the sense of control their perspective gave them.

Granted, this sort of big-picture thinking takes time to develop. But after a few months of eating low-fat, energizing carbohydrates such as beans, fruits, vegetables, pastas, rice, potatoes and whole-grain products, you'll be able to achieve it, too—if you're open to it.

Try reduced-fat fare. It's true: Eating low-fat alternatives to fatty foods such as margarine, sour cream and salad dressings won't actually diminish your desire for the full-fat originals because your mouth will remain accustomed to the feel of fat. But you can still nibble on reduced-fat fare to help get you started on the antifat crusade. Simply use lower-fat substitutes as "transition foods" before weaning yourself from the fat sensation entirely. You may require a little more time to make the taste switch using this method, but you may also be more likely to see the dietary change through.

> THE LONGER YOU CHEW, THE MORE TIME YOUR BRAIN HAS TO ABSORB FOOD ODORS. AS A RESULT, YOU MAY TRICK IT INTO THINKING THAT YOU'RE CONSUMING MORE THAN YOU ACTUALLY ARE.

As for reduced-fat foods, many are downright disappointing. Some low-fat cheeses, for example, are undeniably unappealing. Others, however, are surprisingly delicious. Just be persistent until you find some that you like. Experiment by conducting at-home taste tests and give your palate ample time to adjust. And be open-minded; a different taste isn't necessarily an inferior one.

Follow your nose. Surprising as it seems, neurologist Alan Hirsch, M.D., director of the Smell and Taste Treatment and Research Foundation in Chicago, has found that people who sniff food odors lose weight more readily than those who don't. In fact, the more his study participants sniffed (the range was 18 to 185 sniffs of a variety of foods per day), the more weight they lost. Some even lost too much weight!

While Dr. Hirsch isn't altogether sure why the heavy sniffers lost weight, he postulates that food odors somehow trick the brain into feeling satisfied. "We know that 90 percent of what we call taste is actually smell," he says. "So maybe it's the odors of fatty products that we crave, not the high-fat foods themselves."

Of course, food sniffing isn't a realistic strategy for the average Joe or Josie. But the basics behind Dr. Hirsch's theory certainly are. Try a few of the following scent-related techniques:

- Inhale deeply before you eat.
- Chew your foods well. The longer you chew, the more time your brain has to absorb food odors. As a result, you may trick it into thinking that you're consuming more than you actually are.
- Eat foods when they're hot. They're more aromatic than cold foods.
- Eat fresh foods whenever possible. They're generally stronger-smelling than their prepackaged counterparts.

Keep a food diary. Needless to say, keeping track of what and when you eat is essential for permanent weight loss. Unfortunately, this task is often easier said than done. Research indicates that most of us dieters greatly (albeit unconsciously) underestimate the amount of food we eat each day, perhaps by as much as 800 calories. What's more, it gets even worse. Apparently, the more we consume, the more we forget what we've eaten.

> **W**E DIETERS GREATLY UNDERESTIMATE THE AMOUNT OF FOOD WE EAT EACH DAY, PERHAPS BY AS MUCH AS **800** CALORIES.

The solution? Start a food diary. Purchase a small, pocket- or purse-size notebook and use it to keep track of all of your daily meals—snacks, spreads and salt included. Be sure to write down every item you eat when you eat it.

And don't worry about counting fat grams and calories; you know what's fatty and what's not. A quick evening examination of what you've eaten during the day will clue you in to where your biggest fat bites are—and whether and when you're kidding yourself.

Believe that you can. Becoming a low-fat eater is similar in one very significant way to performing in the Olympics: Both require great mental strength. Consider speed skater Dan Jansen, who won a gold medal in the 1,000-meter race at the 1994 Winter Olympics in Lillehammer. According to sports psychologist Jim Loehr, Jansen didn't care for the 1,000; he preferred the 500. But he conquered the longer race in part by telling himself he loved it—over and over and over again.

Mind over matter—that's the key. If you actually believe that you can change your attitude toward fat, you will; if you don't, you won't. So repeat this mantra to yourself every day: "I control what I eat. I can and I will start eating low-fat foods. I like low-fat foods." It may be one of the oldest tricks in the book, but it works. So why not try it?

—Nancy Monson

Part VI
The Fast Track to Fitness

Best Ways to Whittle Your Waist

The perfectly executed tummy crunch, along with sensible grazing and a few soothing mantras, will have that gut deflated in no time. Here's how.

What you have going with your tummy is a classic love-hate relationship. You love it because it's a part of your body. At the same time, you hate the fact that there's so much of it to love.

You've exercised. You've dieted. And still there's that belly saying "I love you. I will never desert you." And the mere mention of dessert is enough to drive you out of your mind.

Maybe you should consider a tummy tuck. No, we're not suggesting surgery just so you can once again see your toes without sitting down. But we are suggesting that you give yourself a natural tummy tuck. It's a simple operation that you can perform yourself. It's an operation that has nothing to do with scalpels and everything to do with making a few simple but highly effective changes in the way you think, eat and ex-

RESHAPE YOUR LIFE A LITTLE, AND YOU CAN RESHAPE YOUR BELLY A LOT.

ercise. We say: Reshape your life a little, and you can re-shape your belly a lot. Here's how.

Build a Muscle Girdle

In the graceful days of yore, women achieved wasp-waisted perfection by submitting to corsets strung so tightly that breathing was the stuff dreams were made of. What they didn't know was that some well-developed abdominal muscles would have achieved the same thing—and still al-lowed them the habit-forming pleasure of breathing on a regular basis.

"So many women are under the misconception that if you exercise your abdominal muscles too much, they'll get bulky and add a rather masculine girth to the waist," says Ken Cooper, M.D., founder and director of the Cooper Aerobics Center in Dallas. "This just isn't the case."

TONING THE ABS HOLDS IN THE STOMACH.

As a matter of fact, just the opposite occurs. "Toning the abdominal muscles reduces your abdominal girth by virtue of the fact that the muscles are a little bit tighter and can hold in the stomach a little better," says Rudolph Leibel, M.D., associate professor in the Laboratory of Human Be-havior and Metabolism at Rockefeller University in New York City. "It's like putting on a tighter belt."

But before you hit the floor in a mad frenzy of body-flopping crunches, heed this advice: If you want to do it right, do it slowly. "People tend to perform exercise move-ments quickly and get them done in any way their bodies will let them," says Jillian Hessel, a fitness trainer who uses the Pilates Method in her workout programs. "But often that is not the most efficient way of developing the mus-cles properly." The Pilates Method is firmly grounded in the concept of paying almost Zen-like attention to each muscle as you perform a series of gentle exercises very slowly and very correctly. One of the bonuses of this method is that your body can't cheat you by using muscles that it shouldn't be using.

"When people are performing sit-ups or crunches, for example, I see a lot of them doing what I call the pigeon poke," says Hessel. "That's when they tighten their neck and throat muscles and poke their heads forward to initiate the move rather than drawing from the abdominals. Others rely on their hip flexors. But cheating a bunch of fast reps this way isn't going to do your abdominals much good."

To really tighten and tone the upper abdominals, try some slow, well-executed abdominal crunches. With your knees bent and your arms either crossed over your chest or at your sides (instead of behind your head), start by practicing exhaling and pulling your abs in. Then try to curl off the floor using only your abdominals, exhaling on the way up and inhaling on the way down. Do not pigeon-poke your head forward. Curl up as slowly and smoothly as possible. The less you rely on momentum to carry you forward, the more you rely on your abs.

To make the exercise more effective, be careful not to let your stomach pouch out on the upward motion, says Hessel. It helps to keep a hand placed on your lower abdomen, so you can immediately feel when that bulging out is happening. If you find that it always happens at a certain point in the movement, you may want to curl up only to that point until you've developed enough abdominal control to go farther.

Now the big question. To get a truly gut-tightening workout, just how slowly should you be performing your crunches? "I'd say that you want to go for a count of two during the upward, or concentric, phase of the motion," suggests Michael Pollock, Ph.D., director of the Center for Exercise Science at the University of Florida College of Medicine in Gainesville. "But on the way down, the eccentric phase, stretch it out to a count of four."

Most people tend to pay more attention to the lifting part of the crunch and then quickly flop back to the floor. "But they end up missing out on the most effective part of the movement," says Dr. Pollock. "It's during the eccentric phase, when you're lowering your torso to the floor, that real muscle-toning gains are made." So keep it slow.

IT'S DURING THE ECCENTRIC PHASE, WHEN YOU'RE LOWERING YOUR TORSO TO THE FLOOR, THAT REAL MUSCLE-TONING GAINS ARE MADE.

That's the form. Here's the schedule. "I recommend that people work their abdominals at least three days a week," says Dr. Pollock. "But when it comes to the number of repetitions you should be performing, remember this: It's better to do 25 slow crunches with good form than to do 50 fast and bouncy ones."

Try starting with 10, then add 5 a week until you reach 25. Just be sure to keep each curl slow and controlled. "If you're losing your form and speeding up, it means you're tired. Stop," says Dr. Pollock.

To zero in on the lower part of the abdominal muscles, Dawn Gillis, fitness director at Skylonda, a fitness retreat in Woodside, California, suggests this exercise: Lying flat on your back with your knees bent and feet flat on the floor, place your right foot on your left knee. Contract your abdominals, lift your feet off the ground and tilt your pelvis slightly by contracting your buttocks muscles and flattening the small of your back so that your hips come about one to two inches off the floor. Then lower your hips and feet. Exhale as you contract the muscles and inhale on the release. If you need extra support for your back, place your hands, palms down, under your buttocks. Remember to keep the movements small and controlled. And hold those abs in.

Stroll before Dinner

During a study at the Cooper Aerobics Center, researchers asked three groups of women to walk three miles a day, five days a week. One group walked the distance at a heart-pumping 12-minute-per-mile pace. The second group walked at a not-too-shabby 15 minutes per mile, while the third group ambled along at 20 minutes per mile.

Guess which group burned the most fat overall?

"We were as surprised as anyone to find that it was the slowest group that lost the most body fat," says John Duncan, Ph.D., chief of clinical applications at the center. "And they lost the most despite the fact that the 12-minute-per-mile walkers burned 53 percent more calories!"

One of the possible explanations developed at the center is that the intensity of the exercise may dictate the kind of fuel your body burns. "While this is still hypothetical, I like to think of what happened in terms of the high- and low-octane gas you find at a filling station," says Dr. Duncan. "Carbohydrates are a high-octane fuel, while fat is definitely a low-octane one. It stands to reason that if you are performing high-intensity exercise (that is, driving your body like a race car), it's going to utilize high-grade fuel."

Likewise, if you're simply rolling along like a golf cart on a sunny afternoon, your body can use the low-grade stuff—fat.

"Another possible explanation, or one that might work in tandem with the first, is that for the initial 20 minutes of any workout, you don't burn fat. You burn glycogen, a carbohydrate fuel," adds Dr. Duncan. "And if you think about it, the slowest group spent a total of 60 minutes exercising, with 40 minutes of that in the fat-burning mode, while the fastest group spent a total of 36 minutes working out, leaving only 16 fat-burning minutes."

So if you want to lose the fat not only from your belly but also from all over, sustained low-intensity exercise seems to be your best bet. "I recommend four to five times a week, working your way up to an hour," says Dr. Duncan.

> **I**F YOU WANT TO LOSE THE FAT ALL OVER, SUSTAINED LOW-INTENSITY EXERCISE SEEMS TO BE YOUR BEST BET.

And what time of day might be best for taking this leisurely stroll? "I have to fight constant weight gain just like everyone else," says Dr. Cooper. "But I'm proud to say that I'm only three pounds heavier than I was when I graduated from school, and part of my secret is working out before I eat my dinner."

Indeed, research suggests that a predinner workout is an excellent appetite suppressor. "It makes me thirsty, but it's hard to be real hungry when your metabolism is still up."

Graze the Day Away

You'd think that the main reason some people get pot-bellied while others remain annoyingly lean is that the latter bypass fatty foods while the former swim in them. Right?

Maybe not. Where obese people tend to really differ in their eating habits is at breakfast and dinner. "The vast majority of overweight people are far more likely than thinner people to skip breakfast and get at least half, if not three-fourths, of their daily caloric intakes after 6:00 in the evening," says James Kenney, R.D., Ph.D., nutrition research specialist at the Pritikin Longevity Center in Santa Monica, California. "The problem is that the body seems to be a little more efficient at storing fat in the evening than earlier in the day. And it doesn't help that after a big dinner, most people just sit around, watch television and then go to sleep."

OVERWEIGHT PEOPLE ARE FAR MORE LIKELY THAN THINNER PEOPLE TO SKIP BREAKFAST AND GET AT LEAST HALF OF THEIR DAILY CALORIES AFTER **6:00** IN THE EVENING.

It helps to spread the calories evenly throughout the day, although that doesn't give you permission to have a big breakfast, a big lunch and a big dinner. "What happens after a big meal that's high in fat and refined carbohydrates is that your body puts out an excess of insulin," Dr. Kenney says. "Unfortunately, extra insulin prevents your fat cells from releasing fat into the bloodstream, where it can be picked up by other tissues and burned. Excess insulin also turns fat cells into magnets for the dietary fat that's absorbed into your bloodstream after a typical high-fat meal."

In other words, higher postmeal insulin levels more efficiently lock up your fat stores—so much so that it would be easier to melt an iceberg at the North Pole than to melt off an ounce of your potbelly. Higher insulin levels also stimulate the appetite, which leads to increased food intake.

But not to worry. Here's one simple word to keep your insulin level at a low, controlled, fat-burning rate all day: Graze.

Grazing is an invitation to eat moderate amounts of low-fat, high-fiber fare all day long—for instance, a modest breakfast, a little midmorning snack, a modest lunch, a little midafternoon snack and a light dinner.

"It's not necessary to consciously eat less than you did before," says Dr. Kenney. "But the amount you're eating at any given mealtime is less. And the smaller, more frequent meals reduce the amount of insulin produced, which results in less fat stored and more fat burned."

Of course, grazing doesn't work very well if it's based on a daylong progression of high-fat, refined carbohydrates such as candy bars. Go for the baked potatoes, whole-grain pretzels, vegetables, whole fruits, hot cereals, whole-grain pastas, hearty bean or lentil soups—you know, those low-fat, high-fiber foods that are every tummy tucker's standbys.

Relax, Relax, Relax

It may be that the only thing a growing tummy likes better than a piece of cheesecake the size of Manhattan is an oversize case of stress. And the reason is quite simple. Stress causes the adrenal glands to produce adrenaline and cortisol, two hormones that together may behave like tiny moving men when it comes to shifting fat from all over your body into your abdominal region.

"During a stressful situation, adrenaline causes fat cells from all over the body to squirt their contents into the bloodstream," says Redford B. Williams, M.D., director of the Behavioral Medicine Research Center at Duke University Medical Center in Durham, North Carolina. "Once in circulation, those free-floating fat molecules can provide the body with the extra energy it needs to meet the physical demands of whatever situation you're in."

This reaction was just fine for prehistoric people, who needed that extra energy to either run from something with more teeth than they had or fight someone trying to turn their private caves into boardinghouses. But the stress-inducing situations we face in today's world are rarely solved by fighting or fleeing. So those fat molecules coursing through your bloodstream remain unused.

Except maybe for when the cortisol kicks in.

A study conducted at Yale University put two groups of overweight women through a series of stress-inducing tests. The overweight women who sported most of their additional bulk around their middles produced more cortisol than the women whose fat was concentrated in their hips and thighs.

> UNCONTROLLABLE STRESS MAY FAVOR REDISTRIBUTION OF FAT TO THE ABDOMINAL REGION.

"We've been able to show that uncontrollable stress in rats not only increases their levels of cortisol production but also seems to favor redistribution of fat to the abdominal region," says Marielle Rebuffe-Scrive, Ph.D., of the psychology department at Yale. "But this research in women is the first study that actually shows the possibility of the same correlation in humans."

Also, it's known that human adrenal glands affected by serious disease can sometimes excrete more cortisol, and some people affected this way tend to gain weight in the belly.

So it may be that when stress hits, adrenaline unleashes fat from all over your body, and then cortisol sends a considerable amount of the unused portion of fat to your abdomen for safe storage. "It could be that the cortisol chooses the abdomen because it's close to the liver, making that fat more available for quick energy later," speculates Dr. Williams.

An interesting explanation, but hardly cause for celebration if you're looking to tuck your tummy. But here's something else to think over: There's some preliminary evidence that meditation, a favorite stress-reducing technique, may cause cortisol levels to go down.

You may not be able to get rid of all of the things in your life that cause stress. But this research holds out the promise that with a good relaxation technique, you may be able to neutralize stress's girth-growing effects. "We really suspect that controlling stress might make a difference," says Dr. Rebuffe-Scrive. "In addition, controlling stress may help your dieting and exercise efforts."

If you already have a favorite stress reduction technique, use it. "Whether it's meditation, biofeedback, yoga or whatever, all formal relaxation techniques lead to a common set of changes in the body, one of which is to dampen the stress-induced production of cortisol," says Herbert Benson, M.D., chief of behavioral medicine and president of the Mind/Body Medical Institute at Deaconess Hospital in Boston.

So relax already.

—Mark Golin with Michele Stanten

Exercise Your Options

Getting stale? Give your exercise routine a fun change of pace—and put some bounce in your step—with these cross-training moves.

Some walkers are utterly impassioned. They firmly believe that walking is the only fitness activity. Running, they say, is too high-impact, swimming doesn't burn enough fat, aerobic dancing requires too much coordination, and tennis doesn't build endurance.

Well, they may not be wrong, but this unwavering devotion can keep these walkers unnecessarily earthbound. Those who never venture down other fitness avenues miss out on the chance to develop a balance between aerobic and anaerobic conditioning. Between linear and vertical movement. Between muscle toning and muscle building. They miss out on the chance to become the best walkers they can be.

In addition, they miss out on the playful side of fitness. Think about it: Sports such as tennis, volleyball and golf are called games for good reason. There's something intrinsically childlike about playing with a ball. And who doesn't feel like splashing when slipping into a pool, even if it's to swim laps? Certainly, walking is a carefree activity, but when the days are longer and the breezes feel warm and fresh, maybe it's time for walkers to loosen up, kick up their heels and break the gravitational pull that holds them tight.

Before you scream "Heresy!" let us make it clear that we are by no means suggesting that you subjugate your walking routine or imperil your joints. Just add in something new—occasionally. Many people report feeling more enthusiastic about their primary forms of exercise when they mix in other kinds of sports and conditioning. In addition, aspects of fitness not directly impacted by walking, such as flexibility, hand-eye coordination and upper-body strength, can be addressed by varying your training.

TUNE INTO THE PLAYFUL SIDE OF FITNESS.

Variety balances out the fitness equation. Some exercises, such as swimming and tennis, supplement the skills and strengths that walking doesn't touch, while others can simply make you a better walker.

Bounce in Your Step

You'll get a different perspective on fitness by playing with it. Not only will you have fun adding a new element to your fitness regimen, but you will enjoy testing your body by seeing what it can do. Maybe you remember when you couldn't walk a few blocks without getting winded. Now a half-mile is your warm-up. Cross-training is a playful way to prove your strength and fitness.

There are also training and health reasons for introducing new elements into your routine. Left to his own devices, even the most motivated exerciser tends to become physically complacent. We reach a certain level of difficulty and then tend to coast.

This pattern is explained by an exercise physiology theory called Selye's general adaptation syndrome. When your body is confronted with a stress stimulus such as exercise, its first reaction is shock, and you experience soreness. The second phase is adaptation. Your body gets used to the stimulation, and performance improves. Your pace gets faster, your endurance increases, or you can lift more weight.

> **L**EFT TO HIS OWN DEVICES, EVEN THE MOST MOTIVATED EXERCISER TENDS TO GET PHYSICALLY COMPLACENT.

But then comes the inevitable third phase: staleness. Your body is no longer being challenged by the same stimulus. It has learned to do whatever you're asking it to do more efficiently and with less effort. No improvement is experienced. In fact, during this phase, performance may actually decrease unless there is a change in stimulus.

To keep up your fitness level, it's important to vary your program periodically, either in intensity or in the type of training you do. By spicing up your fitness program with weekly sets of tennis, biweekly runs or a game or two of golf, you'll be able to rise above the plateau.

For a Well-Rounded Workout

To help you become athletically well-rounded, we consulted with experts in five sports—tennis, golf, swimming, running and volleyball—and asked them to recommend one exercise that would benefit walkers. The result is this "mini-circuit" of six exercises that will build strength and coordination as well as provide muscular balance.

Tennis. Grab a racquet if you want to improve your agility, hand-eye coordination, anaerobic power and lateral movement.

This exercise, the side lateral jump, is courtesy of Nancy Miller and Patrick Fagen, court conditioning experts at Athletic Performance Programs in Lake Tahoe, California. It effectively works the inner and outer thigh muscles, helps balance and adds explosive power in the lower body.

Stand with your feet shoulder-width apart, your knees slightly bent and your weight on the balls of your feet. Your hands should be in front of you in a comfortable position. Your chest and head should be up. Crouch down and spring off your right foot, moving directly to your left and covering as much distance as you can. Land with your left foot first, then your right, making sure to land on your toes so as to minimize impact. You'll be in the starting position, only a few feet to the left.

Immediately spring back to your right in a continuous lateral jumping pattern. Gradually work up to three sets of 20 lateral jumps (10 to each side).

Golf. Tee off if you want a strong midsection and upper-body range of motion.

This trunk flexibility exercise—also a subtle strengthener—is offered by Michael Wook, an Arlington, Massachusetts, personal trainer and expert on sport-specific conditioning.

Lie on your back with your knees bent, your feet flat on the floor and your arms out straight in a T to stabilize your body. Keeping your shoulders on the ground, let both knees drop to the right. Be sure to keep your knees and ankles together. Perform the movement slowly. Return to the starting position and drop your knees to the left.

Perform 25 repetitions per side.

Swimming. Swim some laps if you want endurance, upper-body strength and a nonimpact workout.

The wall push-up, from Gerry Rodrigues, 1992 Masters Coach of the Year, is an all-around upper-body strengthener that can be done almost anywhere.

Stand at arm's length from a wall. Put your arms straight out, placing your palms on the wall. Now step back 6 to 12 inches. Your arms should be straight but angled downward somewhat; if they're not, move them down an inch or so. In this position, do a push-up against the wall. Lower your body by bending your elbows, making sure you keep a flat back. When your face is about to touch the wall, straighten your arms and return to starting position. Work up to three sets of 12.

Running. Run a mile if you want improved endurance and leg strength.

We turned to Bob Esquerre, fitness director of Equinox Fitness Clubs in New York City, for these two overall leg strengtheners that will enhance your roadwork, whatever your speed.

Attach the two straps of a Powerband around your ankles. (The Powerband is available from Phil Tyne, 14999 Preston Road, Suite 212–286, Dallas, TX 75240; 1-800-295-8943.) Lie on your back with your legs straight out. Flex both feet. Bend your right knee and bring your right heel as close to your buttocks as possible, with the foot still flexed. Keeping that heel fixed there, lift your straightened left leg about four to five inches. Lower and repeat, working up to 15 repetitions. Switch legs and repeat.

Next, extend both legs straight out. Keeping your feet flexed, draw your left heel toward your butt as far as possible. Then extend your leg back to the starting position. Perform up to 15 repetitions per leg, alternating sides.

Volleyball. Spike a volleyball if you want hand-eye co-

ordination, explosive power
and quick feet.

For muscular balance in the
lower legs, Mark Cibrario, of
the Multiplex Fitness Center in
Deerfield, Illinois, suggests the
toe raise. Activities such as vol-
leyball and walking target the calf muscles, while this exercise strengthens the tibialis anterior, the long muscle on the
front of the lower leg.

SPIKE A VOLLEYBALL IF
YOU WANT HAND-EYE
COORDINATION, EXPLOSIVE
POWER AND QUICK FEET.

Stand with your feet comfortably apart. Flex your feet,
pulling your toes toward your shins. Keep your weight on
your heels. Lower your toes and repeat. Do three sets of 15.

Borrowed Moves

In the pursuit of fun and games, adopt a casual approach. There's no need to train like Steffi Graf or to shoot
under 100 in golf. Instead, join a volleyball league that's or-
ganized by your local YWCA. Pick up your walking pace
to an easy run for part of a workout. Take golf lessons at
a public course or sign up for court time; golf and tennis
offer great "quality time" for couples or friends.

In addition to improving your health and body by
playing these sports, you can reap fitness benefits by borrowing moves and exercises from them. By performing
moves from other sports, you link the chain of muscles and
skills that are essential to being fit all over.

Do the set of exercises described in this chapter two or
three times a week after your walks, or incorporate the exercises into your walks. To do this, start off on your regular
walk and then stop after about five minutes to do an exercise, such as the side lateral jumps or wall push-ups. After
completing each exercise, resume walking for a few more

minutes and then stop for another spot-exercise break.

Whether you try seven sports and 15 new exercises or just add a few strengtheners to your workout, the important thing is to have fun while staying fit. Ultimately, you'll be a better walker and a healthier person.

—Jonathan Bowden and Sarah Bowen Shea

Making a Splash

Sore knees? Aching back? Tired feet? You can take a load off and get a workout with soothing water exercises.

Exercise can be hard on your body. When you run, for example, a force three times your body weight comes crashing down on your foot with each stride. This pounding adds up over time, and it may lead to injuries.

How can you avoid this punishment? You may want to hit the water. Water exercise is much easier on your body, because in shoulder-deep water, the water supports 90 percent of your weight. This means no pounding, even during intense exercise.

People with arthritis have known for years that water exercise pampers sore joints. It also provides a gentle yet fitness-producing workout for women who are pregnant, people with heart problems or multiple sclerosis and the elderly.

Besides preventing injury, water workouts can:

• Increase motion in your joints almost painlessly, because the water supports your limbs. If

you have arthritis, working your joints may help you maintain mobility.
• Increase your fitness by challenging your heart and lungs—if you exercise vigorously.
• Improve your strength. Because of water resistance, moving your limbs through the water works your muscles more than on land. The faster you move, the greater the resistance.
• Add fun and variety to your exercise program.

So find a pool or another body of water that has convenient hours and isn't too crowded. Water around 80° to 85°F will feel most comfortable. Then try any of the water exercises described below.

Hydro High Jinks

If you went swimming as a kid, you probably jumped in the water, frolicked about, splashed your sister and didn't stop until Mom or Dad dragged you out hours later. You had loads of fun, and in doing so, you got a lot of great exercise.

That was exercise? Yes. Simply having fun in the water burns calories and contributes to health. (But drifting on a raft doesn't count!) Playing without a specific workout in mind can also help you work off stress and refresh you.

Splash Dance

Water aerobics classes are similar to regular aerobics classes. With a leader demonstrating the moves, pupils push, pull, leap, kick, twist, turn and get a great workout. Injury risk is low, because your body weight is supported by the water.

But no exercise is foolproof. Because of the freedom of

Water Workout Do's and Don'ts

When you shift your exercise from land to water, it's important to continue following commonsense exercise principles.

- Always warm up before exercising vigorously. Stretch before and after workouts, holding each stretch for several seconds. Never bounce.
- Gradually increase your exercise intensity over several minutes.
- Practice good technique. Don't, for example, risk straining your calves (by running on your toes) or your back (by leaning as you run).
- Beware of dehydration, just as on land. Drink plenty of water before and after exercise.

movement allowed in the water, it may be tempting to push movement further than you should, and you hurt yourself. So listen to the instructor and use common sense (see "Water Workout Do's and Don'ts").

Aqua Walking

Because of water's resistance, walking in water will burn more calories than walking on land at the same speed. You'll burn more calories in shoulder-deep water than in waist-deep water as your upper body fights resistance. You can burn even more energy in shoulder-deep water by swinging your arms. Holding plastic water dumbbells or partially filled plastic jugs adds even more resistance (see "Pool Toys You Can Use" on page 171).

Using different strides will work different muscles and

add variety. Mix forward strides with backward and side-ways strides. You can point your toes, go heel first, raise your knee to your chest or kick your leg out before each step. Be creative.

Aqua Running

Water at least waist deep will best support you as you turn around in the water. Waist-deep to chest-deep water means your feet push off the bottom as you run. You can add intensity by picking up the pace or raising your knees. Another approach is to tie yourself to a large object at pool-side and run in place (see "Pool Toys You Can Use").

Water deep enough to keep your feet off the bottom can also provide high-intensity training. While you run, a flota-tion vest or belt will help keep your head above water.

Getting Serious

Water exercise offers a great edge for serious exercisers. Water tires you out as it protects your body. Water work-outs allow you to:

- Enhance performance by working on your speed (sprint or interval work) without risking injury
- Experiment with and hone various running styles be-fore trying techniques on land
- Mix water workouts with regular workouts for variety and to give your joints and muscles a break
- Exercise hard while injured
- Use leg weights and other means to increase fitness without increasing the pounding force on your legs

As with any workout, water exercise can have draw-backs. You may need to fight boredom, especially when exercising in place. And in deep water, since you don't

Pool Toys You Can Use

A line of fancy equipment often accompanies a new activity. Water exercise is no exception. Often, however, everyday objects can substitute for high-tech equipment.

- Plastic water dumbbells add resistance to your hands and arms as they move through the water. Partially filled one-gallon plastic jugs held underwater are another option.
- Plastic "doughnut" ankle cuffs add resistance to leg movements. An old pair of sweatpants for walking in shallow water can do the job, too.
- Shoes cushion and protect your feet. Options range from specialized footgear to old tennis shoes.
- Flotation devices will buoy you during deep-water exercise. You can buy specialized a vest and belt, or you can use a life jacket.
- A tether secures you to a large object at poolside while you exercise in place. You can fashion a tether using nylon rope tied to a bicycle inner tube, which goes around your waist.

support your body weight, exercise can become almost effortless. In either case, you need to constantly push yourself. Some athletes forgo flotation devices for harder workouts.

Gauging how hard you're working can be tough in water. Try to keep a pace similar to on land. Relying on your pulse rate to tell you how hard you're exercising may not work, since water pressure slows your heart rate. Instead, listen to your body. A hard workout will make you feel tired, whether in or out of the water.

Tiring out early can also be a problem. Movements in

water may be unfamiliar and take more energy. Try to find a comfortable pace.

To maximize enjoyment, choose water exercises that most interest you. You may want to alternate wet workouts with dry ones—or you might have so much fun, become so fit and feel so good in the water that you'll never go back to land!

—Bryant Stamford, Ph.D., director of the Health Promotion and Wellness Center at the University of Louisville and an editorial board member of Physician and Sportsmedicine

Muscle Out Fat

The path of most resistance—weight training—can build muscle and reduce belly fat at any age.

For many of us, middle age hits most notably around the middle. The waist widens and the tummy gives under the weight of an ever-expanding mass. But packing on excess pounds is just half of the problem. Even if our scales haven't budged much over the past 20 years, what was once muscle may have been replaced by fat. And fat around the abdominal organs is believed to balloon the risk of heart disease, diabetes and certain kinds of cancer.

But don't despair. You can get back your 25-year-old body at any age. What it takes is a regimen that includes vigilantly adhering to a healthy low-fat, low-calorie, high-fiber diet, dedicating at least 45 minutes a day to fitness walking or some other moderately vigorous aerobic activity and, perhaps most

YOU CAN GET BACK YOUR 25-YEAR-OLD BODY AT ANY AGE.

important, embracing a program of resistance training.

The latest research suggests that dusting off the dumb-bells and using them may replace fat with muscle, even if you're past age 60. In this study, 13 men around 60 got rid of about four pounds of fat and built about four pounds of muscle while following a resistance-training program for an average of four months.

The guys liked their tighter looks and extra energy. But it took more than that to impress the researchers. They looked at where the men lost the blubber and found that almost half of the fat that scrammed was the potentially dangerous central-body fat. Yet-to-be-published research suggests that resistance training could give older women the same good deal.

"Older people have more to gain by beginning a resis-tance-training program," says study author Ben F. Hurley, Ph.D., director of the exercise science lab at the University of Maryland at College Park. "Younger people have greater reserves of muscle and strength, beyond the amount required to maintain everyday activities. But as we age, strength training becomes more important, because many older people become sedentary and start to lose valuable muscle."

> **T**HE MORE MUSCLE YOU HAVE, THE QUICKER YOUR METABOLISM, AND THE EASIER IT IS TO KEEP POUNDS AND INCHES AT BAY.

Appetite's Best Friend

While aerobic workouts are still the most efficient way to burn calories and reduce your fat stores, resistance training is the key to building up your active muscle tissue for long-lasting increases in metabolism. The more muscle you have, the quicker your metabolism, and the easier it is to keep pounds and inches at bay.

Age is no barrier to building your body's calorie-burning furnace. In fact, one study found that elderly people in a resistance-training program required about 15 percent more calories than they needed during their sedentary days just to maintain their weight.

The Workout to Muscle Off Fat

Want to get back where you belong—and perhaps even look better than you did at age 25? We asked Daniel Kosich, Ph.D., senior consultant to IDEA: International Association of Fitness Professionals, to design a resistance workout to complement a healthy diet-and-aerobics routine and to help you look toned, trimmed and proportioned. We also requested that the workout be easy to follow, whether or not someone belongs to a gym.

Some of these exercises are most effective when done with dumbbells. If you haven't been working out with weights, first try the exercises without any. Then add a 1- or 2-pound set of dumbbells and gradually work your way up to 5, 10 or 15 pounds for some of the exercises. To squeeze the most from your efforts, Dr. Kosich advocates using the principle of progressive resistance: Work each muscle to the max by doing each exercise until you can't do any more using good form. Build up to the maximum number of repetitions and sets given next to each exercise below, then move up to the next heavier weight and build up from the beginning again. Keep all of the exercises slow and controlled, and rest about one minute between sets. Do this workout two to three times a week.

Push-up. An excellent workout for your chest, your shoulders and the backs of your arms, push-ups don't require weights and can be modified for most anyone. If you are really out of shape or have bad knees, start by doing them against a wall. Facing the wall, stand about arm's length away and place your palms on the wall. Now bend your elbows, lower yourself toward the wall and then push yourself back to the starting position. Don't worry if your heels come off the floor a bit.

Otherwise, start with your knees on the ground. Place your hands on the floor slightly more than shoulder-width apart. Be careful not to arch your back. Holding your tummy in helps. Keep your eyes to the ground to maintain your neck in a neutral position. Do as many push-ups as you can in this position, working up to two sets of 25. When you've mastered these, you may want to switch to a straight-legged position (toes and hands on the floor) for an added challenge.

Pull-up. Pull-ups work the biceps and the latissimus dorsi, the long muscles that line the sides of your back and create an attractive V-shaped body when toned. You'll need a bar or a portable bar that adjusts to fit the doorways in your home (available in most sporting goods stores). Keep your hands slightly wider than your shoulders. Do these with your palms facing you for an effective biceps workout. Beginners should put a chair beneath and to the side of the bar to boost themselves into the starting position. Begin with your chin above the bar. Now lower yourself until your elbows are just slightly bent. Then using the chair, boost yourself up to the starting position and repeat. As you get stronger, you'll be able to pull yourself up without using the chair. Pull-ups are tough, so don't get discouraged. Just do as many as you can, eventually working up to one set of five to ten.

Crunch. Crunches tone your abdominal muscles. Lie on your back and keep your knees bent, feet flat on the floor. Lift your upper body until your shoulder blades are just off

Wired for a Workout

We don't know whether it has charms to soothe a savage breast, but there is evidence that music may boost your workout.

Twenty-six people pedaled longer on stationary bikes when working out to music than when cycling to just the rhythms in their heads. Men moving to music increased their time on the bikes by almost 30 percent, and women were able to go about 25 percent longer before feeling exhausted.

All subjects exercised to the sounds of their own choosing—mostly rock 'n' roll for these college-age subjects. But there's nothing magic about rock, says study co-author Esther Haskvitz, Ph.D., assistant professor of physical therapy at Springfield College in Massachusetts; the key is choosing something you enjoy hearing.

These researchers didn't turn up any new connection between music and muscle that prolongs endurance. "The effect may have been due mostly to the distraction of the music," says Dr. Haskvitz. Although this study did not test it, she says that listening to the radio or to informational tapes may help a workout as well. For some people, knowing that they'll get the news may not only boost their time to exhaustion but also motivate them to get moving in the first place.

the floor, then lower. Cross your hands over your chest or put them behind your head, but don't pull against your head—let your abdominals do all of the work. Hold your head in a neutral position (not crooked forward or back). You should be able to fit your fist between your throat and chin. Work up to two sets of 25.

Squat. Squats shape the fronts and backs of your thighs as well as your buttocks and calves. They are most effective when done with dumbbells held at your sides or resting on your shoulders. Stand with your feet slightly wider than your shoulders and slightly turned out. Begin with a partial squat, knees bent at about 45 degrees. Do as many as you can, working up to three sets of 12. Progress to a 90-degree squat (knees bent at right angles, so you feel like you're lowering yourself into a chair). Keep your abs tucked in and your back straight. If you have a history of knee problems, check with your doctor to make sure you can do this and the following exercise without straining these joints.

Lunge. Lunges also work all of the muscles of your legs and buttocks. Start with one foot in front of the other, about three feet apart. Lower your back knee toward the floor, then come back up. Keep your front knee aligned over your front foot to make sure you bend your knee no more than 90 degrees. Don't lean forward—your torso should drop like a plumb line. You can hold on to a chair for balance. Repeat with the other knee in front. Work up to three sets of 12, alternating legs.

Then progress to the more advanced step lunge: Starting with your feet together, step forward with one foot, drop your back knee straight toward the floor, then press up with your front leg and return to starting position. Repeat with the other leg stepping to the front. Keep the movement slow and controlled to prevent straining your knees. You can add a pair of dumbbells at your sides or resting on your shoulders for more resistance.

Supine fly. These work the chest and the fronts of the shoulders. Lie on your back on a bench, with your knees bent and your feet on the bench to keep you from arching your back. Start with light weights. With your elbows slightly bent, extend your arms out to your sides at right angles to your body, as though you were hugging a barrel.

Then keeping your elbows bent, bring your arms in over your chest until the weights just about meet. Maintain the tension in your chest and shoulders to control the movement back down. Work up to one to three sets of 12.

Prone reverse fly. These work the upper back and the backs of your shoulders. Lie on your stomach on a bench, turning your head to the side. The weights should hang from your hands below the bench. Pull the weights straight out to your sides by squeezing your shoulder blades together; your palms should be facing downward. Do not jerk the weights. Work up to one to three sets of 12.

Seated lateral raise. These strengthen and shape the shoulders. Sitting on a chair, hold weights at your sides. Lift the weights straight out to your sides until your hands are at shoulder height, keeping a slight bend in the elbows. As you raise and lower the weights, your palms face the floor. Work up to one to three sets of 12.

Arm and leg raise. These strengthen the lower back. Lie on your stomach on the floor, arms overhead. Turn your head to one side. Slowly lift your right arm and left leg straight up, then lower. Repeat using your left arm and right leg. This is a small movement. Press your hips and shoulders to the floor to keep from rotating. Work up to one to two sets of ten on each side, alternating sides.

—Jan Bresnick and Marty Munson with Michele Stanten

Walk It Off Your Way

Whether you're a spurter or the long, leisurely type, you can peel pounds by marking miles.

Envious of the pounds melting off that neighbor who walks for 45 minutes every day? Just because you don't have that kind of time doesn't mean you can't walk weight off, too. Keeping in mind that your body, your temperament and your time schedule are different from your neighbor's, we're going to talk you through four different walk-it-off programs.

Focus on one or try them all (after checking with your doctor, of course). Alternating methods won't diminish their effectiveness, and it may keep you from getting bored or burned out. That's essential even after the weight is lost. "Your weight loss should be permanent as long as you maintain your walking routine and healthy eating habits," says Peggy Keating, fitness director at the Duke University Diet and Fitness Center in Durham, North

Carolina. So here are some doctor-recommended ways to make the walking habit stick while the weight goes away.

Walking in Water

If your back or knees hurt, and if a walk to the end of the driveway seems difficult, try walking in a pool first.

Walking in waist- to chest-deep water allows you to gain muscle strength and endurance while protecting your joints from excessive stress and strain. When you feel stronger, try some short walks outdoors or in a mall. Or vary your routine: Try one day of weight-bearing exercise such as walking, then one day of non-weight-bearing activity such as stationary cycling, water walking or swimming, says Terri Merritt, exercise physiologist at the Preventive Medicine and Research Institute in Sausalito, California. Not only does the change keep your exercise program interesting, it also decreases the risk of overuse injuries, which can come with doing weight-bearing exercise every day.

> **W**ORKING OUT UP TO SIX OR SEVEN DAYS A WEEK IS GREAT IF YOU'RE TRYING TO LOSE WEIGHT.

Always pay attention to what your body says to you. And don't expect fast results; that only backfires. Losing more than a pound or so a week is too much.

Taking your workout up to six or seven days a week is great if you're trying to lose weight, says Merritt. How do you know if you're overdoing it? "Overfatigue, joint pain, a heart rate that doesn't return to less than 100 beats per minute within ten minutes after exercise. An hour or two after walking, you should feel like you can carry on with your normal activities and not be too tired," she says.

LSD Walking

If you hate working up a sweat and you have the time, long, slow distance (LSD) walking is a great way to work out and burn calories. You'll burn approximately as many calories as someone going at a faster pace, as long as you cover the same distance. And you're much less likely to get injured or strained.

LSD walking means putting aside 45 to 60 minutes five to seven days a week. But don't plan a long route on your first day out! If you've been inactive, start with as little as 5 to 10 minutes a day and slowly work your way to the 45- to 60-minute goal. That might take as long as three months.

Eventually, you'll need to plan one or several routes that are three to four miles long. For a while, you may want to use a route that never goes too far from home, so you can drop out and go back if you get too tired. Always keep your pace moderate, so you can go the distance without pooping out.

Walking in Spurts

For the very busy person, or for those who are too out of shape to walk for long, consider walking for short periods of time throughout the day. For example, you could walk 10 minutes in the morning, 10 minutes at lunch and 10 minutes after dinner instead of one 30-minute walk.

IT'S THE TOTAL CALORIE DEFICIT AT THE END OF THE DAY THAT REALLY MATTERS, NOT HOW FAST OR SLOWLY YOU WALK.

"We used to feel that LSD was the best way to walk for weight loss, because it seemed that the body burned fat preferentially during long bouts of exercise," says Susan Johnson, Ed.D., fitness-walking expert at the Cooper Institute for Aerobics Research in Dallas.

Add Weight for Extra Burn

Walking, running and bicycling are all great aerobic exercises that burn fat. But if you want to boost your calorie burn all day long, our experts agree that training with weights for 20 to 30 minutes two or three times a week is part of the price of the ticket. Walking tones certain muscles, but it doesn't make up for the constant muscle loss that everyone experiences as they age. Several of our experts spoke from personal experience.

"When I added weight training, I was amazed at the difference. I could eat more and still maintain my weight," says Peggy Keating, fitness director at the Duke University Diet and Fitness Center in Durham, North Carolina. "We used to believe that aerobic training was the only way to lose weight. And people were told not to bother with strength training until they had already lost weight. Now we know the opposite is true. We encourage our clients to start building muscle, in addition to their aerobic training."

"But now we know that's not the only way." It's the total calorie deficit at the end of the day that really matters, not how fast or slowly you walk.

"I suggest that people work up to two sessions of 15-minute walks or three sessions of 10-minute walks seven days a week," says Dr. Johnson. This gives your body a metabolic boost two to three times a day. Depending on how you're tuned, this might work better for you than exercising once for a long period, she says.

Interval Walking

People who have plateaued in their weight loss or who have just a few pounds to shed might do well to turn to interval training. Dr. Johnson cautions that this is reserved for people who want to lose about 20 pounds or less, who don't mind working up a sweat, who want to get the most calorie burn per minute from their walks and who are fit enough to walk several miles at a brisk pace.

> **I**NTERVAL TRAINING IS FOR PEOPLE WHO WANT TO GET THE MOST CALORIE BURN PER MINUTE FROM THEIR WALKS.

It's simple. Plan to walk for 20 to 30 minutes or more. Start out by walking at a comfortable pace for 3 minutes, then walk briskly for 1 minute. Walk comfortably hard, but don't strain. After a week or two, walk moderately for 2 minutes, then briskly for 2 minutes. After another two weeks, walk moderately for 1 minute and briskly for 3 minutes. Walking at a moderate-to high-intensity pace may increase your calorie burn during and after exercise, compared with what low- to moderate-intensity walking does.

"But," you say, "if I get out of breath, won't I be burning carbohydrates instead of fat?" Yes, but that's okay. It is not the type of fuel your body is burning but how much you burn that may matter.

If you don't love interval training, you don't have to keep it up forever. "Once you've reached your goal weight, you can relax a little," says Dr. Johnson. "As long as you maintain some sort of regular fitness routine and healthy eating habits, you'll keep the weight off."

—Maggie Spilner

Part VII

Tame Down the Tension

Ten Surefire Stress Stoppers

Arm yourself with these tension-taming tactics to avoid stress-induced food binges.

Let's face it: We all get a little stressed out once in a while. The car breaks down, a check gets bounced, a deadline is missed. Fortunately, these are usually isolated incidents, and when the crisis ends, our brows unfurrow, our breathing slows, our fists unclench, and life goes on, relatively free from tension. At least that's the way it's supposed to work.

But sometimes the first crisis is followed by a second . . . and a third. And it's this type of prolonged stress that can run you down, create bags under your eyes, lead to overeating and, worst of all, shorten your life span.

In fact, virtually every organ in your body can be negatively affected by too much stress. And the consequences reach far beyond fatigue, puffy eyes and an expanding waistline. "The more stressed you are, the more likely you are to experience illness—particularly heart disease," says Nancy Frasure-Smith, Ph.D., associate professor of psychiatry at McGill University in Montreal who conducted a study of the effects of stress reduction on heart disease patients. What's more, the higher your stress level when you have a disease, the less likely you are to survive it.

Now here's the good news: You can stop the stress and, in doing so, keep the nervous munchies under control. As a bonus, taming tension may also lead to a longer, healthier

THE CONSEQUENCES REACH FAR BEYOND FATIGUE, PUFFY EYES AND AN EXPANDING WAISTLINE.

life. In Dr. Frasure-Smith's study, cardiac patients who were monitored for stress and given tips on reducing it were 50 percent more likely to survive than patients who didn't get such help. A mere six hours of contact with nurses, who calmed patients' fears and answered their questions, was all that was needed to make the difference between life and death.

Fortunately, you don't need the help of a reassuring nurse in order to relax. You need to just arm yourself with a few tension-taming tactics. Here are ten that the experts recommend.

1. Lean on a friend. Open up to a loved one about your troubles. Share your hopes, dreams, needs and frustrations. And allow others to do the same with you. Psychologists believe that such intimacy not only immediately reduces stress but also provides loving, nonjudgmental support, which will help give you the confidence you need to deal with your setbacks—including dietary indiscretions—in a positive manner.

2. Say a prayer. This can be a very effective way to evoke the stress-relieving relaxation response and to focus attention away from food. The following relaxation method is taught to patients by Herbert Benson, M.D., chief of behavioral medicine and president of the Mind/Body Medical Institute at Deaconess Hospital in Boston: Find a quiet place and sit comfortably. Choose a soothing word or phrase, then repeat it over and over in your mind. "Eighty percent of my patients chose a word or prayer associated with their faith, even though they were offered the choice of another soothing word, such as *peace* or *ocean*," says Dr. Benson. And those people who used words related to their religion stayed with the program longer and improved their health more than those who used nonreligious terms.

3. Soak your cares away. A warm bath can make stress go right down the drain. Experts say that warm baths help alleviate tension not only by relaxing your muscles but also by slightly heating your brain, which can be calming. The temperature of the bathwater should be comfortably warm to the touch—between 100° and 102°F. (If the water is too hot, it can shock your system and cause your muscles to constrict.) And if you have a heart condition, be sure to limit your soaking time to 15 minutes or less; longer tubbing could cause your blood pressure to drop, and you could faint.

4. Get a dog . . . or a cat . . . or a fish. Pets are faithful friends who will listen to your troubles without interrupting or offering bad advice—and they may even be able to save your life. Research has shown that heart attack victims who have pets live longer. What's more, watching a tankful of tropical fish may lower blood pressure, at least temporarily. Also, pets may relieve stress by bringing out your more playful side and making you smile. And having a pet that needs walking is guaranteed to get you moving, whether you "want out" or not.

5. Laugh it off. If you're caught in a situation that you can't escape from or change, humor may be the healthiest form of release from your temporary stress. During the laugh itself, your heart rate and blood pressure rise slightly, after which there's an immediate release: Your muscles relax, and your blood pressure sinks below prelaugh levels. A good giggle may also prompt the brain to emit endorphins, the same stress-reducing chemicals that are triggered by exercise. And a hearty chuckle can even help fight illness by temporarily boosting your body's levels of immunoglobulin A, a virus-fighting antibody.

6. Let the band play on. Maybe it's the rhythm, or maybe it's the melody. Whatever the reason, music helps

HAVING A PET THAT NEEDS WALKING IS GUARANTEED TO GET YOU MOVING, WHETHER YOU "WANT OUT" OR NOT.

relieve stress. Studies show that music played for patients before, during and after surgery seems to decrease the feelings of surgery-associated stress by reducing the number of stress hormones secreted in the brain. And slow music played during meals can help you eat more slowly and savor every bite, so you feel satisfied without seconds.

7. Picture a tranquil scene. Dew shimmers on rose petals at sunrise. Waves lazily roll onto a steamy tropical beach. Although scientists don't yet know why, envisioning pleasant scenes such as these can help you become the picture of tranquillity. One study revealed that hospital patients whose rooms overlooked trees recovered faster than those who viewed brick walls.

If you don't find yourself in or near any real-life tranquil settings, try gazing at a photograph of one. Then focus on enjoying the serenity of the setting just as you would if you were there. Besides calming you down, such visions remind you that there's more to life than food.

8. Take a hike. Your body reacts to stress as if you were in danger, releasing biochemicals to prepare your body to fight or flee. This makes your body more easily store calories as fat. To get rid of these biochemicals, you need to get moving—in essence, to flee.

That's where walking comes in. Walking instantly helps dissipate these chemicals—while it burns calories.

But you don't have to wait for stress to strike to hit the high road. You can also take a stroll to avoid a stressful situation or to clear your mind before facing an inevitable one. Or when at work, take a walking break instead of a snack to reinvigorate yourself.

9. Breathe easy. "Deep breathing is one of the simplest yet most effective stress management techniques there is," says Dean Ornish, M.D., director of the Preventive Medicine Research Institute in Sausalito, California, and author of *Eat More, Weigh Less*. Breathing deeply works by infusing the blood with extra oxygen and causing the body to release endorphins. It has effects far beyond the quick-fix sugary snacks we often eat to relieve stress.

To take a relaxing breath, slowly inhale through your nose, expanding your abdomen before allowing air to fill your chest. Then slowly exhale. Practice this for a few minutes each day or whenever stress strikes.

10. Focus your attention. Allow your mind to become fixed on a pleasant sight, sound or smell. It can be the sight of clouds floating by, the sound of a bird singing outside or the scent of a flower. Focus on the image, sound or smell, allowing your mind to be free from all other thoughts for a few minutes. Be sure to take time for a few such mental rest stops throughout the day.

—Nick Bosco

Calm Your Mind, Tone Your Body

High in the California redwoods, find the peace and the pace that lets you effortlessly drop pounds.

The knock on the door signals that it's time to get up. It's Dawn (she's the fitness director) making her predawn rounds. The clock reads 5:30, but fresh off a flight from the East Coast, my body says it's 8:30; jet lag never felt so good. Time for a flash shower, then on with the sweats. Downstairs, the stretch class is beginning. For 45 minutes, we gently twist and stretch amid yawns and groans. Daylight gradually streams through the trees, streaking across the room.

Breakfast beckons us to the dining room. I can hardly believe the size of it! A huge bowl of perfectly cooked oatmeal topped with a piquant raisin-and-prune sauce and a crumbling of no-oil granola, with a few almond slivers. To my surprise, I easily devour every spoonful.

Not much time to spare. We gather our fanny packs, fill our water bottles, lace our hiking boots and climb into a van. A ten-minute drive delivers us to our first hike of the day: a postcard-perfect redwood forest.

"What's that sweet smell?" asks Marcus, an East Coast urbanite.

"Fresh air," his friend quips.

We all chuckle, but indeed, the air is delicious.

Welcome to Skylonda

So begins Day One at Skylonda. Located about 20 miles south of San Francisco on Skyline Boulevard, not far from the little town of La Honda (hence the name), this fitness retreat attracts people as much for its promise of spiritual renewal as for its physical challenges.

Weight loss, though not emphasized in any of Skylonda's literature, is practically inevitable, given the design of the program. Key to the experience is hiking ten miles every day on some of nature's most scenic trails and feasting on California's tastiest 10-percent-of-calories-from-fat food this side of the Dean Ornish program.

> NO OUNCE OF EXCESS CAN HIDE AS THE TAPE MEASURE ENCIRCLES MY CALVES, THIGHS, HIPS, WAIST, CHEST AND UPPER ARMS.

Does it matter that I've hiked only twice in my life—and that was years ago? Is a 40-minute treadmill workout three times a week enough to prepare me for eight hours of fairly vigorous exercise six days in a row?

The president of Skylonda, Dixon Collins, assures me that I'll be fine. "Don't worry. You'll be surprised at what you can do," he says.

To establish fitness levels and monitor gains (and losses) throughout the week, check-in begins with a basic fitness assessment and measurements that are taken first in pounds, then in inches.

No ounce of excess can hide as the tape measure encircles my calves, thighs, hips, waist, chest and upper arms.

Calipers pinch here and there to determine my percentage of body fat. Angles measure my hip flexibility. A heart rate monitor strapped across my chest and a blood pressure cuff wrapped around my arm establish my cardiovascular fitness while I pedal a stationary bike.

Woods Words

Out on the trail, Dawn divides us into two groups according to our fitness levels. Each group has at least two trail guides, equipped with cellular phones and first-aid kits, to lead and sweep. (That's trail-speak for bringing up the tail end.) Our group takes the high road. We climb steeply through low-growing huckleberries under a canopy of redwoods. Then the trail levels out as it contours around a ridge. The path is narrow, but we talk back and forth, getting acquainted.

Bruce, a Miami businessman, joins me for a short time; then his long, experienced hiking legs pull him ahead. Stu, a San Franciscan, shares his favorite eateries with Hillary, a New Yorker who will be staying overnight in San Francisco before flying home. Marcus suddenly erupts with a piercing mock call of a macaw.

Meanwhile, markers along the way announce that we've gone two, three, four, five, six miles. I'm amazed at how quickly we've covered ground.

Bushed, we return to the lodge, where a batch of blueberry smoothies—some kind of sweet electrolyte replacement concoction—awaits us. The break is short-lived, however, as we are hustled along to the circuit-training class.

The Ultimate 30-Minute Workout

I've never seen equipment like this before—kind of sleek, with no cumbersome weights strung along their spines. Dawn explains that each of these machines delivers resistance by way of a fluid-filled hydraulic cylinder. As you pump, the fluid in the cylinder is forced through an aperture. The resistance is simply a product of how rapidly and forcefully you pump. Dawn demonstrates: With one finger, she slowly lifts a lever arm. There's almost no resistance. Then she jerks the lever arm hard and fast, and the machine resists like a ten-pound weight.

Called progressive aerobic circuit exercise (PACE), this offers the ultimate workout—so they say. The nice thing is, you don't have to stop to adjust the resistance; depending on how fast you pump, it automatically adjusts to your effort.

Each of us hops on a machine and gives it a try. Like weight-training machines, each of these is designed to work a certain muscle group. Arranged in a kind of circle alternating with aerobic platforms or steps, stationary bikes or stair-climbers, the machines are poised for a circuit-training session. The music begins, and we all get pumping to the aerobic beat. After just 30 seconds, Dawn bellows "Change," and we move to the neighboring piece of equipment. We continue for 30 minutes, changing stations every 30 seconds. Raining sweat, all of us look like we're having fun.

Cooldown follows. Then we move outdoors to the green for a half-hour of floor (or rather, turf) exercises focusing on the abs. Ugh. I didn't know there are so many different ways to tone a tummy.

Is It Lunch Yet?

We have a 15-minute break. I check the massage schedule posted by the front door. Lucky me: I have a massage next—gotta skip aqua-aerobics. I down a glass of water, grab a handful of carrot sticks and rush downstairs to the spa. Robert greets me, and for the next 60 minutes, I surrender my muscles to him. This is the day's sole scheduled hour of pampering, and I'm relishing every second.

Afterward, somehow I feel lighter.

Cuddled in a terry-cloth robe and slippers, I float up the stairs to the dining room. People are just beginning to gather for lunch.

Even if I hadn't worked up such an appetite, I would not leave a single morsel of lunch on the plate. *Mmm*—grilled chili-rubbed turkey breast and black-eyed peas served over an assortment of baby lettuce leaves with a tangy dressing. I'm almost tempted to have seconds, but instead, I pluck another slice of crusty whole-grain, home-baked bread from the basket. With a cup of decaf in hand, I head out to the deck to read and relax a little before the next round of vigorous activity.

The pause passes too quickly. It's back to the gym for another 30-minute PACE session, then floor exercises (this time concentrating on the legs). After a quick change and blister fix, we're off on the 4:00 hike. Thankfully, this trail is shorter than the one we hiked this morning, though it includes some hill climbing.

Four miles later, at the end of our trek, we stop to pay homage to Methuselah. Fourteen feet in diameter and 1,800 years old, this is one of the oldest living redwoods on the peninsula. Talk about longevity.

From Silence to Sharing

At Skylonda, 6:00 signals quiet hour. Time to meditate, nap, veg out or do whatever we have the energy for—as long as we do it silently. Exhausted, I head to the sauna.

I don't expect anyone to dress up for dinner. And no one does. Liberated from street clothes, makeup, jewelry, even blow-dried hair, we've adopted ease and comfort as our new priorities. Clean sweats conveniently double as dinner attire.

(continued on page 198)

Lose It Fast, Make It Last

Most quick weight loss (more than 1½ pounds per week) almost never lasts. That's because most get-slim-quick schemes rely on caloric deprivation, a doomed-to-fail ploy for several reasons. First, very low calorie diets wear thin real fast; nagging hunger and low energy make them nearly impossible to maintain. And even if you could, you should not, because sharp calorie cuts (below about 1,200 calories per day) make it difficult to get all of the nutrients necessary for a healthy diet.

These diets aren't only bad for health, they're also bad for weight loss. That's because the body equates less food with famine and goes into an energy conservation mode, operating more efficiently on fewer calories. This may sound good, but it makes it more difficult to lose pounds and encourages weight gain when you go off the diet. In fact, subsequent gains frequently outweigh the losses.

By contrast, a body-slimming program like that offered at Skylonda sends pounds packing with no return ticket. Here's how.

More Food, Fewer Calories

Meals and snacks are carefully calibrated to keep daily caloric intake comfortably around 1,400 for women and 1,500 for men, explains Timi Gustafson, R.D., consulting nutritionist for Skylonda. But no one gets hung up on calorie counting. Guests who aren't interested in losing weight are free to double-dip into the breadbasket or request second helpings.

Overeating is naturally limited by diet composition, she explains. At 70 percent carbohydrates (mostly from whole grains, fruits and vegetables), 20 percent protein and 10 percent fat, with a minimal amount of sodium, the diet is designed to supply lots of quick energy for the day's activities and about 30 to 35 grams of fiber, which gives the feeling of fullness usually provided by fat.

Still, guests are often amazed at how much they are eating. Some insist they are eating more than they do at home—which is quite possible, because you get more food for fewer calories when you eat high-carbohydrate, low-fat fare.

Burn, Burn, Burn

"The average person is in motion six to eight hours a day," notes Skylonda's fitness director, Dawn Gillis. And every activity is geared to maximize the fitness-building and fat-burning effect.

Even the resistance-training component of the program, called progressive aerobic circuit exercise (PACE), utilizes a unique hydraulic system that works the body aerobically, too.

"A 30-minute PACE workout burns as many calories as a 25-minute aerobics class, with the added muscle-strengthening benefit of a 25-minute weight-training session," claims Ray Manz, Ph.D., a representative of PACE equipment. "It's a very efficient way to burn fat and build lean muscle tissue."

A 30-minute circuit strength-training program burns more calories—and elevates postworkout metabolic rate—better than almost any other 30-minute exercise program, agrees *Prevention* fitness adviser Wayne Westcott, Ph.D., national strength-training consultant for the YMCA.

The other advantage of the PACE workout is that it's gentle on the muscles and doesn't cause soreness, so Skylonda guests can participate in two sessions a day.

As a result of this and the other activities, people burn calories like crazy—roughly 3,000 to 4,000 a day.

It takes a 3,500-calorie deficit to drop a pound of body fat. Considering the caloric intake and energy expenditure during a one-week stay (six active days) at Skylonda, it's no mystery how guests can lose three pounds of body fat.

And once again, the food is unbelievable. It starts with grilled Japanese eggplant with a miso-and-garlic sauce, which is followed by tofu with a banana-ginger sauce. Amazing fare!

After a glorious dessert of poached pears, we shuffle upstairs and gather around the huge stone fireplace in the great room. Neil, Skylonda's mind/body specialist, sits on the raised hearth stroking a gnarled stick that's decorated with multicolored streamers, like a miniature maypole.

"This is our talking stick," he explains. "It's a symbol of sharing, much like a peace pipe. When people come to a retreat like Skylonda, they usually come for a reason. We're going to ask you to share with us why you've come and what you hope to leave with at the end of the week."

With that, he lays the streamer-covered staff in the middle of the table and entreats each of us, as we feel the urge, to pick up the stick and speak.

No one speaks. Neil sits quietly, as if meditating. As the minutes pass, the silence becomes heavy with anticipation. Will anyone pick up the stick? What if no one does? How long will we sit here?

What seems like 30 minutes passes. Finally, Marcus takes the wand. "I am living with an illness that may very soon take my life," he begins.

The silence envelops him.

"The strange thing is, I've never been happier, because I'm finally doing what I've always wanted to do. In fact, that's why I'm here. Skylonda is on my to-do list. I've always wanted to hike in the redwoods."

He lays the talking stick back on the table. There is a brief pause, as we all try to comprehend. We have all been touched. Somehow, I feel my perspective on my own life shift. Then one by one, without hesitation, each person passes the stick.

Hiking the Inner Path

Midweek, the hike takes an introspective twist. At the head of the trail, we wait our turns. Then one by one, at several-minute intervals, each of us sets out on a solitary hike. With no one to walk (or talk) with, we're free to set our own paces and follow our own mental wanderings.

Except for a few instances—when a switchback trail reveals another hiker, for example—I feel peacefully alone. Of course, there is comfort in knowing that fellow hikers are just paces ahead and behind. And there's no denying the security of having Todd flag every intersection or fork in the road, so we won't veer off course.

I glide through a shady grove. Then as I emerge into the sunlight, the dense vegetation gives way to a spectacular view across the canyon. A couple of hawks soar below. I take a deep breath, filling myself with the experience.

The narrow dirt trail follows the canyon rim for a while, then begins a gradual descent through thickets of wild rose and flowering scrub. My mind drifts in and out: One moment I'm intent on a salamander scurrying across my path; the next I'm contemplating the events of the past week. Slowly, my thoughts evaporate, and the landscape gently lulls me into a trance.

> **S**LOWLY, MY THOUGHTS EVAPORATE, AND THE LANDSCAPE GENTLY LULLS ME INTO A TRANCE.

Moments—or perhaps miles—later, raindrops awaken my awareness. I look overhead and see a cloudless blue sky beyond a dense redwood canopy. The "raindrops," I discover, are falling from the trees, their needled branches dripping with moisture. The trail becomes softer underfoot now and is fringed with forget-me-nots and redwood sorrel. Ferns cascade down the hillside. A tiny bird flits by, lilting the sweetest song. I notice the faint sound of rushing water, and through the mist, I see a stream.

Amazingly, while I was lost in my thoughts, the trail led me to this mystical rain forest.

I continue to follow the path down to the stream strewn with moss-covered boulders and across the wooden bridge. Then I begin my ascent up the other side. For a while, the lush tropical environs prevail. But gradually, as I climb higher, the cool humidity dissipates, and the trail becomes decidedly steeper. I'm really sweating now.

Of necessity, my breathing switches from automatic to manual. I inhale deeply, then exhale vigorously through my mouth with a whoosh. The rhythm helps propel me forward. But it feels like the grade is getting steeper.

Our trail leader warned us that the last 2 miles of this hike are all uphill (after 4½ miles of level or gradually descending grade). I stop to catch my breath, but only for a couple of seconds; then I push on uphill. My body and mind pull together to meet the challenge. I try taking longer strides and pumping my arms for propulsion. Walking backward—something I learned on the steep sidewalks of San Francisco—makes the going easier. But I quickly realize it's too treacherous on this rugged terrain.

So I enlist every visualization technique Dawn taught us the day before. First, I pretend that I have a towrope in hand and go through the motions of pulling myself up the hill. Then I imagine pushing off giant springs with each backswing of my arms. The techniques seem to work for a bit.

As I approach a bend in the road, I hallucinate that the end is just around the curve. It isn't. The seemingly endless trail snakes its way ever upward.

Now my mind taunts me. "You're not going to make it," it whispers. I glance backward and remind myself how far I've come. With optimism restored, I climb on.

Finally—I can hardly believe it!—the van is in view. Exhausted as I am, I feel strangely exhilarated.

Emotionally and Physically Lighter

From Wednesday on, the week slips away, mile by mile, conversation by conversation, one wonderful meal after another. I've gotten so accustomed to living in sweat suits and terry-cloth robes that I can't imagine wearing street clothes again. But I will—just as soon as the last tape measurements and group photos are taken.

> OUR FINAL "GRADES" ARE IN, AND EVERYONE IS PLEASED. I LOST FOUR POUNDS AND FOUR INCHES.

Friday night is reserved for the talking stick. Neil asks us to share our achievements from the week. No one mentions pounds dropped. Many speak of emotional baggage shed. The week has had a positive, if not profound, effect on almost everyone. There was lots of well-wishing for Marcus, who left early to catch a hot-air balloon across the Napa Valley—another check on his to-do list.

Saturday morning, after a sunrise hike with an incredible panoramic view, we return to breakfast. Our final "grades" are in, and everyone is pleased. I lost 4 pounds and 4 inches. My roommate, Chris, lost no weight but dropped 11 inches. Two of the biggest "winners" lost 5.5 pounds and 9 inches and 4 pounds and 13.5 inches, respectively. Of the 13 people who submitted to final measurements, the average weight loss is 3.38 pounds and 8.2 inches—almost 3 inches from the middle (waist and abdomen) alone! Not bad for a week's work.

—Emrika Padus

Strategies for Super-Stressed-Out Days

Stop overeating and other stress-related problems before they start with this energy-saving schedule.

Your company's annual audit is just weeks away, which for your department means longer hours, shorter lunches and taking work home. But this year, there's something else. Your 12-year-old is rehearsing for her first ballet recital. She's counting on you to watch her practice—and to drive her to and from evening rehearsals. The grandparents are flying in to see her. And they're staying with you. All of this in a two-day period.

Energy is a precious commodity in today's world, especially for double-duty women struggling to fill challenging roles in competitive workplaces and bustling families. Even those who easily handle most busy weeks can find themselves worn and frazzled when the heat is really on.

There's no foolproof recipe for keeping energy high, concentration sharp and mood bright, but the experts are full of ideas that can help you take the panic out of pressure. Endurance is a matter not so much of finding new energy as of making the most of resources you already have.

Key point number one: Be prepared. "It's better to prevent stress-related problems than to clean up the mess when you are already overloaded," says research psychologist James Campbell Quick, professor of organizational behavior at the University of Texas at Arlington.

If you know the crunch is coming, honestly assess what help you're going to need and arrange to get it. Maybe your spouse or children can take over some of your customary home duties for a few high-stress days. Or enlist a friend, perhaps suggesting an exchange when the tables are turned.

> **A**SSESS WHAT HELP YOU'RE GOING TO NEED AND ARRANGE TO GET IT.

On the physical level, there's abundant evidence that good conditioning boosts endurance. If you haven't been exercising, get into training. Just two weeks on a moderate walking program is enough to build stamina, says D. W. Edington, professor of kinesiology and director of the University of Michigan Fitness Research Center in Ann Arbor. Start with whatever is comfortable—as little as 5 minutes a day—and work up to at least 45 minutes a day. (Even as little as 15 to 20 minutes a day offers some benefit.) In addition, find opportunities for activity whenever you can.

So you can meet the challenge ahead, it's also crucial to learn energizing techniques that you can use during your high-stress time. To provide you with lots of effective strategies and guidance on how to use them, we consulted experts across the country and gathered 48 hours' worth of energizers targeted for specific times of the day.

Day One: Eating for Daylong Energy

6:30 A.M. Arm yourself with an endurance-energy breakfast by choosing foods that break down slowly and keep blood sugar levels steady, says Richard Podell, M.D., author of *The G-Index Diet* and clinical professor of medicine at the University of Medicine and Dentistry of New Jersey Robert Wood Johnson Medical School in Piscataway. He recommends, among other foods, "compact carbohydrates," whose structures are dense and don't break down as easily as those of other carbohydrates. They include pita bread, pastas and most vegetables.

Foods that digest quickly, such as flaky cereals, muffins and most breads, which crumble into pieces that are quickly broken down, give your blood sugar a boost that drops two to four hours later, leaving energy flat, says Dr. Podell.

A high-energy breakfast should include a protein (low-fat or skim milk, low-fat or nonfat yogurt or an egg), citrus juice or a fruit (with the exception of pineapple, watermelon and raisins, which are high in sugar) and a compact carbohydrate such as coarse oatmeal (not instant) or a high-fiber bran cereal.

Take a multivitamin/mineral supplement with breakfast. Stress increases the rate at which your body excretes some vitamins and minerals, such as magnesium and the B vitamins.

Consider jump-starting your day with caffeine, but budget your intake. If you overindulge, you may be too jumpy to concentrate, or you may feel draggy later. Caffeine concentrates energy but doesn't create it, says Quentin Regestein, M.D., director of the sleep clinic at Brigham and Women's Hospital in Boston: "It's like borrowing money from the bank. You walk out with a full wallet, but eventually, there's payback."

7:00 A.M. Delegate some of your responsibilities. Ask your spouse or children to take over some of the day-to-day household chores, such as preparing meals and washing dishes.

8:00 A.M. Before you launch into your day's work, make

a list. Once your tasks are down on paper, you won't have to worry that you'll overlook something.

10:00 A.M. Have a piece of fruit to keep your blood sugar steady.

Noon. Get ready to take a lunch break. Although you may be tempted to skip lunch, it's important to stay as close as possible to your regular eating time. "Many people experience drops in their blood sugar levels and feel tired if they delay or skip meals," says Dr. Podell.

Lunch should be modest (big meals make you drowsy), high in protein and low in fat and sugar. A sandwich of lean meat or fish, plus a green salad, would be a good choice. But pass up the pasta salad. A big dish of starchy food unaccompanied by protein increases the brain's production of serotonin, a neurotransmitter that can make you sleepy. Fat has the same effect.

> **LUNCH SHOULD BE MODEST, HIGH IN PROTEIN AND LOW IN FAT AND SUGAR.**

2:30 P.M. Take a 20-minute nap if you're at home. "Naps can have major recuperative effects on alertness," says Roger Broughton, M.D., professor of neurology at the University of Ottawa. In short naps, restoration occurs without your getting deep sleep, says Dr. Broughton. If you nap for 50 minutes, though, your sleep may be so sound that awakening will leave you groggy.

Naps come easiest and help most during the "nap zone," about 12 hours after the midpoint of the previous night's sleep. If you slept from 10:30 P.M. to 6:30 A.M., for example, your nap zone would be 2:30 P.M.

If you can't take a nap, recharge with 15 to 20 minutes of deep relaxation, says Dr. Podell. Find a quiet spot, close your eyes and visualize the scene that most represents calm and peace to you: a hot afternoon at the beach, for example, or a bracing morning in the mountains. Imagine in detail the sounds and scents.

3:00 P.M. Reward yourself with a pleasant drink, such as juice, soda or regular or decaffeinated coffee. Some people find that mixing half regular coffee and half decaf helps them feel alert without making them wired.

4:00 P.M. Switch gears to get a second wind, says Ellen Langer, professor of psychology at Harvard University. The fatigue you feel plowing through paperwork may surprisingly disappear when you pick up the telephone. That's because turning to something new sparks your interest and makes it easier to concentrate. You're naturally absorbed in the details of the task before you, a state that psychologists describe as mindful. "Mindfulness is energy-begetting," says Langer. What's exhausting is fighting to pay attention while your mind wanders.

5:30 P.M. Choose the right energy booster for the end of the day. You're exhausted, but you still have to prepare dinner, drive your daughter to rehearsal and check with your family about tomorrow's plans—plus you've brought some work home. You may be tempted to load up on caffeine, but many people find that having caffeine after 5:00 P.M. (or, if you're sensitive, after early afternoon) disrupts sleep. And beware of hidden caffeine sources such as some painkillers (check the labels), chocolate and colas, warns Karl Doghramji, M.D., director of the sleep disorders center at Thomas Jefferson University in Philadelphia.

Having a candy bar to boost energy isn't a good idea, either. The sugar rush fades quickly and leaves you depleted. In a study conducted by Robert Thayer, professor of psychology at California State University, Long Beach, young men and women felt more fatigued an hour after consuming sugary snacks. Try a ten-minute walk instead. The California study found that the physical stimulation of a brisk ten-minute walk increases alertness and energy for up to two hours. It also boosts mood and optimism.

6:00 P.M. For dinner, have pasta or another high-carbohydrate dish if you're still feeling stressed. This can help you relax naturally.

9:30 P.M. Take steps to unwind. The pressure and arousal of being busy up until bedtime is likely to make sleep elusive and fitful. "Give yourself a half-hour to an hour of winding-down time before bed," advises Dr. Doghramji. Do a crossword puzzle, read a book (one that's not too exciting) or listen to some favorite music. Avoid alcohol: You may drift off easily after a few glasses of wine, but your slumber won't be as deep or restorative.

You can also try a stress buster. Even if you're normally a sound sleeper, unusually high levels of stress can keep you awake. The following might be helpful:

- A warm bath 20 to 30 minutes before bed. "This has a real muscle-relaxing and sleep-promoting effect," says Dr. Broughton.
- A warm beverage such as herbal tea or milk. It stimulates a nerve in the stomach that sends a message to the brain, inducing sleep, according to Dr. Broughton.
- Tapes that feature relaxation exercises or the soothing sounds of nature.

10:30 P.M. Go to bed at your usual time. Even if you must sacrifice some sleep to finish a task, you're better off rising early than staying up late. A delayed bedtime shortens deep sleep and disrupts body rhythms, much the way jet lag does.

Although we all differ, most of us can get by with one to two hours' less sleep than usual for a few days, says Dr. Broughton. If you sleep less than five hours, however, you'll definitely feel it. "We know that most deep, recuperative sleep occurs during the first four to five hours," says Dr. Broughton. "Reduce sleep beyond that point, and you're cutting into the most important component."

Day Two: Eating for Peak Performance

You're into the homestretch of your super-stress period. Day Two of the plan includes more tips, plus some strategies designed to help you function at your peak during a three-hour crunch period in the afternoon.

6:30 A.M. Have a high-protein, high-complex-carbohydrate breakfast, such as two ounces of low-fat cheese, a slice of whole-wheat pita bread, one cup of orange juice and a half-cup of skim milk.

10:00 A.M. Have a snack of plain (or artificially sweetened) low-fat or nonfat yogurt.

Noon. Eat a light lunch, such as cantaloupe with low-fat cottage cheese.

1:30 P.M. to 4:30 P.M. During this crunch time, try these tactics.

• Fill your mug with coffee or tea unless caffeine makes you nervous. This may be the best time to get an energy jolt.
• Set your priorities, then take the short view. Instead of yearning for a distant goal—finishing the report, shopping for dinner, attending the ballet recital—concentrate on the column of figures or the task immediately in front of you. Think of yourself as a runner in a long race: If you dwell on all of the miles before the finish, you'll feel overwhelmed. But focusing on the strength of your legs and the details of the landscape as it passes by, moment by moment, keeps energy high.
• Think positive. Try looking back to a time when you mastered a difficult situation, says Debra Nelson, associate professor of management at Oklahoma State Uni-

versity in Stillwater. Also, resist the tendency to "cata-
strophize," says Nelson. "Be
realistic. What are the true
odds that you'll miss your
deadline?" she says.

> **R**ESIST THE TENDENCY TO
> "CATASTROPHIZE." WHAT
> ARE THE TRUE ODDS THAT
> YOU'LL MISS YOUR DEADLINE?

• Make time for at least one
exercise break. Take a stroll or stretch, suggests Edington. Moving your muscles and joints increases blood
flow and sends nerve impulses that stimulate the brain,
he says.

• If you start to feel overwhelmed, pull away. The temptation is to push yourself harder. Instead, "get off the
treadmill," advises Rhoda Frindell Green, a New York
City psychological consultant who specializes in career
and business planning and development. Breathe, relax
and become aware of the thoughts that are making you
anxious.

5:30 P.M. Dedicate the evening to rewarding yourself for
making it through your two-day challenge. When you get
home, tell the kids to hold your calls, then take a long bath
or shower. Instead of cooking, send out for a favorite meal.
Rent a movie you've been wanting to see or start that book
you've been saving. Above all, remind yourself that tomorrow is going to be much easier.

—Carl Sherman

Part VIII

Manage Your Emotions— And Your Weight

Feeding Your Feelings

Most people eat to satisfy their psyches as well as their stomachs. Here's how to manage your emotions—and your weight.

What's more fattening: a dozen chocolate chip cookies or the lonely Friday nights you spend baking them? Large cartons of fries or the squabbles with your mother that prompt you to purchase them? Triple scoops of mint chocolate chip ice cream or the frozen romances that impel you to devour them?

The answer, as you may have guessed, is neither: Foods and moods can be equally fattening.

> **W**E STOPPED EATING FOR STRICTLY PHYSICAL REASONS NOT LONG AFTER DINNER WAS SERVED AT THE END OF A SPEAR.

"Because many of us use foods to satisfy our emotional needs as well as our physical needs, the way we feel often dictates how and what we eat," says Peter Miller, Ph.D., executive director of the Hilton Head Health Institute in South Carolina and co-author of *If I'm So Smart, Why Do I Eat Like This?*

In fact, Dr. Miller estimates that as much as 50 percent of the eating that most of us do is emotionally driven—and highly fattening, because it's not biologically necessary. "We stopped eating for strictly physical reasons not long after dinner was served at the end of a spear," he says. "Today, most of us have the luxury of choosing to eat what we want, when we want and why we want, and about one-third of all Americans are overweight because of it."

But you don't have to be. Often you can regain control of your emotions, your eating patterns and your waistline by engaging in just a little introspection.

The Five Worst Offenders

Some researchers believe that emotional eating is spurred by an innate drive for a certain quota of comfort and pleasure in your life. "When you experience the pain of a negative emotion such as sadness, loneliness or anger, for instance, you may feel the urge to compensate with the pleasure of some favorite food," says Dr. Miller.

Of course, negative feelings aren't the only ones that stir up the appetite. Positive feelings such as happiness can stimulate it, too. "Witness the celebratory gorging that regularly occurs at weddings, birthdays and holiday get-togethers," says Dr. Miller. "We often overeat in these situations as a way of amplifying our positive feelings."

Which emotions do the most dietary damage? Here are the five feelings that experts assert are especially fattening.

Anger. Probably the most fattening emotion of all, says Dr. Miller, anger can trigger overeating in several ways and for reasons that vary with the circumstances. For instance, if you feel as though you've been wronged, you may overeat in an attempt to gain compensation. If your wrath is self-directed, you may overindulge to punish yourself. And if you're upset with a loved one who would prefer that you were thinner, you may overeat as a form of revenge. Regardless of the situation, however, your anger will fill you with excess energy, for which eating becomes a release.

Depression. Are you inclined to overeat when you're depressed? Odds are you're attempting to inject some pleasure and satisfaction into your life through food, says Ronald Podell, M.D., director of the Center for Mood Disorders in Los Angeles and author of *Contagious Emotions.* Problem is, dispirited eaters often end up feeling more depressed after they eat, when the postbinge guilt hits, than they did before they indulged. "And this pattern can lead to even more eating, deeper depression and ever-diminishing self-esteem," explains Dr. Podell.

> **I**F YOUR WRATH IS
> SELF-DIRECTED, YOU MAY
> OVERINDULGE TO PUNISH
> YOURSELF.

Boredom. Like depression, boredom can drive you to the refrigerator in search of momentary pleasure. But if you succumb to the urge too often, it can also drive you toward depression—and excessive eating. "That's why it's important to engage in activities that are motivating, challenging and fulfilling when you're bored or depressed," says Dr. Miller. "You need to boost your self-esteem in these instances, not reduce it even more by remaining idle and eating."

Loneliness. No surprises here: Food provides comfort when you're lonely. Ultimately, however, it prevents you from forming other, more healthful relationships. How? By prompting you to gain weight and grow even more reticent to venture outside your house, where you might actually eliminate your lonesomeness by spending time with friends or meeting someone new.

Happiness. "Many people use food to make them feel even better than they do already," says Dr. Miller. "They don't realize that a little healthful restraint could boost their moods that much more."

Emotional Rescue

Although your past experience may indicate otherwise, you are more powerful than your emotions. You can curb or even curtail an inclination to eat to satisfy your psyche and not your stomach. Here's how to start.

Recognize the pattern. "Building awareness is half of the battle," Dr. Miller asserts. "Once you learn to recognize emotional eating for what it is, you can learn to control it."

To that end, note your behavior during high-risk situations, such as when you're alone, when you're emotionally drained or depressed or when you're attending a party or a reception. If you find yourself inhaling doughnuts or parked by the dessert station, ask yourself two questions: Are you really hungry? And if not, why are you eating? Pausing just long enough to imagine how you'd feel without the momentary solace of a snack can help you identify a tendency to eat out of anger, loneliness or bliss rather than real hunger.

Another helpful trick: Keep a food diary. If you write down exactly what you eat and why, you'll force yourself to become more conscious of your intake and your patterns.

Practice the ten-minute rule. Once you realize you're on the brink of a psyche-satisfying binge, your next step should be to run interference. Try waiting at least ten minutes to see if the urge to eat passes. Ride your bike, fold laundry or take a walk around the block as you wait. Then if you still crave the fattening food, Dr. Miller suggests drinking a tall glass of water to fill your stomach as you continue with your activity. Or you can try one of the other options listed below.

ASK YOURSELF TWO QUESTIONS: **A**RE YOU REALLY HUNGRY? **A**ND IF NOT, WHY ARE YOU EATING?

Are You an Emotional Eater?

The following test, developed by Peter Miller, Ph.D., co-author of *If I'm So Smart, Why Do I Eat Like This?* and executive director of the Hilton Head Health Institute in South Carolina, consists of ten questions that require simple yes and no answers. A total of four yes responses or more indicates a tendency to feed feelings, not hunger pangs.

1. You argue heatedly with your spouse, then leave the house in a huff to dine alone. Does your distress prompt you to eat more than you otherwise would?
2. Your boss tells you at 11:00 A.M. that you won't be receiving the raise you were promised. Does your disappointment impel you to overeat at lunch?
3. You spend an hour trying to program your VCR, only to miss the show you wanted to tape. Is your next stop the freezer and a pint of Ben & Jerry's?
4. You learn that you've earned $2,000 in the stock market. Do you celebrate with a five-course meal?

Find an alternative. Eating isn't the only avenue for reducing anxiety or enhancing pleasure. Reading, walking, jogging, making love, listening to music and lounging in a warm bath can also soothe your soul.

Talk rather than eat. Talking not only occupies your mouth (so you won't eat), it can also help you get to the bottom of what's bugging you in the first place. "Reach for the phone rather than the food in the fridge," recommends Dr. Podell. "By letting out your feelings, you'll be less driven to self-medicate by taking in food."

Satisfy your cravings with healthful, low-fat foods. If you simply must do some munching, then nosh on foods that are low in calories and fat and high in nutritional value. Fresh fruits and raw veggies are your best bets, but

5. You discover that you've lost an unexpected $2,000 in the stock market. Does your depression lead you to Mrs. Fields?

6. You're watching a bodybuilding pageant in which your younger sibling is a finalist. Does your envy drive you to devour a bag of chips?

7. Your five-year-old is finally resting quietly after a bad fall. Do you attack the cupboards for some "pain relief" of your own?

8. You're thrilled to be attending your roomie's wedding. Do you overindulge at the buffet in honor of the occasion?

9. Someone very close to you dies suddenly. Does your grief spur you to eat more than you otherwise would?

10. You find yourself home alone on a Saturday night. Do you order a Sicilian pizza to keep you company?

rice cakes and air-popped popcorn are smart choices, too. (All demand lots of cathartic chomping to swallow.)

Resolve personal conflicts. Iron out your personal problems, which often drive the urge to overeat, and you may be able to curb your tendency to indulge. Confront your overbearing boss or talk with your insensitive friend. But if your attempts at resolution fail or produce more turmoil, ask for help.

Consult an expert. Certain psychological knots are simply too intricate to unravel on your own. So don't hesitate to call in a professional. "An objective opinion can help you make sense of a situation that might otherwise seem hopeless," says Dr. Podell.

—Porter Shimer

Watch Your Words— And Drop Pounds

A language-induced attitude adjustment can steer your thoughts away from food and toward a slim, new future.

Has it ever struck you that losing weight is harder than it ought to be?

I mean, it seems like it should be Arithmetic 101: eat less = weigh less = end of problem. But in reality, it often is more like Astrophysics 901, with the solution receding faster than the edge of the universe.

If any problem needs an alternative approach, it's weight loss. So we're going to look at what we can learn about weight change from a collection of psychological techniques called neurolinguistic programming, or NLP.

Power to Change

Notice that I said weight change, not weight loss. "*Lose* is not a good or positive word in our society," says Doug Sauber, a certified NLP trainer in Philadelphia. "Who wants to lose something? All of the associations are negative. It may even set up an unconscious fear of success. So we talk with people about weight change, which is neutral."

Okay, so that's not exactly rocket science. But at least it shares part of what neurolinguistic means: the relationship between the words we use and the thoughts, reactions and even results they lead to.

But NLP goes beyond words into what neurolinguists call brain systems. It could be, they figure, that people who have great trouble unblubbering themselves are trying to do the job with the wrong parts of their brains.

"I've found that very often it's people with strong receptor orientations—people whose primary orientations are to their feelings—who become overweight," says Sauber. "Because they seek pleasant sensations and emotions in the here-and-now, it can be difficult for these people to resist the temptations of food."

> **W**HO WANTS TO LOSE SOMETHING? ALL OF THE ASSOCIATIONS ARE NEGATIVE. IT MAY EVEN SET UP AN UNCONSCIOUS FEAR OF SUCCESS.

Not that these people are like so many little Roman emperors. Far from it. "They may be extremely caring, even selfless people who are always concerned about how you feel, too," Sauber explains.

"Like nurses are, for instance?" I asked him.

"Yes, exactly."

I had a special reason for bringing up nurses, actually. A leader in the nursing profession had told me that she's eager to have nurses become both teachers and role models for healthy living. But first, she candidly admitted, many nurses would somehow have to overcome weight problems that, for one reason or another, seem all too common among their ranks.

Sauber thinks the connection makes sense. "All day—or night—a nurse is looking out for others. Their priorities are her priorities. And the work can be emotionally painful, too."

The result? These nurses are so busy caring for others that they're not getting the care they need.

"Everyone needs nurturance, especially people oriented to the feeling state. And when their jobs are serving others— both patients and doctors—the need is even more acute. So where does it come from? Food may be an easy answer."

But how does someone with a feeling-first brain train avoid that all-too-easy answer?

NLP says don't fight it; just switch tracks. "You have to learn to get out of that feeling state at least partially, at least sometimes," Sauber explains.

A good way to do this is to focus much more mental energy on making very specific plans and schedules that track you from the present into the future. Make vacation plans. Career plans. Education plans. Exercise plans. Think about them. Visualize them. In fact, see the future unfolding in your mind's eye.

There is more than one reason that this may help, Sauber suggests. First, it helps get your mind off the immediate attraction of food. But second, NLP says, seeing the future actually engages a different brain system—the visual system, in contrast to the feeling system.

Eating things that you know aren't good for you is a feeling-oriented, in-the-moment activity. A person eats a piece of cake because it will feel good to eat it now. Weight change is a future-oriented activity.

Planning for things that bring you personal pleasure and satisfaction may be especially helpful. To help you look at the future, put up some photos of how you want to look one year or maybe 18 months from now. The best photos to emulate are ones showing activities. "How do I get there?" "What's my plan?" Visualize your answers.

The Right Motivator

"Here's a question for you," I said to Sauber. "Some *Prevention* readers tell us that they have used this technique very successfully. But others say that what works for them is not positives but downright nasty negatives: plastic bags filled with lard to represent what they're carrying on their bodies or photos of fat people (maybe even them when they were heavier). So which approach works best?"

"Try both," was the answer. "See which works best."

> **D**IETING IS A FAT PERSON'S ACTIVITY. WHY BE OBSESSED WITH FOOD AND EATING WHEN THAT'S WHAT GOT YOU INTO TROUBLE TO BEGIN WITH?

NLP, you see, strongly believes that people are quite different in what motivates them. Some people are great chasers of dreams, while others are terrific avoiders of nightmares. Whichever best fires up your purpose-in-life pistons, go with it.

As you're looking at your future, NLP suggests that you look up—literally. When you look down, you tend to engage the feeling function of your brain, says NLP. Look up, and you become more visual. You feel better.

Maybe that's why NLP is an alternative approach. Some of its suggestions are, as we say, out there.

Another tip from Sauber: When you make those plans and goals, don't be put off your new track just because you don't reach your goal in the time frame you'd hoped for.

"The whole purpose is not so much to reach the goal but to get you moving in the right direction," he says. "That's what's important."

Sauber is also against the measure-everything-you-eat-down-to-the-gram school. And brutal calorie cutting. "Dieting is a fat person's activity. Why be obsessed with food and eating when that's what got you into trouble to begin with?"

Yes, be conscious of your eating, but don't drive yourself to denial. That will only backfire.

One positive step toward weight loss, by the way, is walking. Schedule it into your daily activities, so you can really take the time to do it. The most pathetic trap is to be so busy doing things for others that you have no time to do things for yourself.

Keep a log. Look at it. Do the visualization thing: There you are, active, purposeful, walking briskly into a healthier future.

—Mark Bricklin with Michele Stanten

The Bad-Body Blues

Is a poor body image keeping you from being trim and slim? Here's how to get out and get moving even when your body isn't perfect.

Laura Myers had always enjoyed being physically active. Throughout her twenties, she frequently ran, biked or went to aerobics classes, all activities that she felt she could do competently on her own. But she dreaded team sports. Whenever other people were watching and counting on her to perform, Myers felt clumsy, inadequate and out of shape.

Over the next couple of years, Myers started in-line skating and skiing with friends—no pressure, just fun. She was surprised to learn that she could keep up with and sometimes even outperform them. She started to feel fit, competent and comfortable with her body. When some co-workers at an office picnic started a volleyball game, Myers jumped in and had a great time. The confidence she had gained in her body's abilities overrode any twinges of self-consciousness she still felt.

If you, like Myers, can conquer your own negative body image, you can move on to greater levels of fitness and athletic performance. Perhaps you are currently exercising, but you don't enjoy it as much as you could because you constantly compare your body with those of other people. Or maybe you've gotten sidetracked because of a busy schedule, bad weather, pregnancy or lack of motivation—and the longer you're inactive, the worse you feel. Even if you're a serious athlete, you can let negative thoughts about your body interfere with physical performance.

> **WHEN YOUR BODY IMAGE IS WARPED, IT CAN PREVENT YOU FROM REACHING YOUR GOALS, FITNESS OR OTHERWISE.**

When your body image is warped, it can prevent you from reaching your goals, fitness or otherwise. "If you can break through that mental roadblock, learn to accept the body you have and reward yourself for what it is capable of, you can use that self-acceptance to reach higher levels of fitness," says Carole Oglesby, Ph.D., a sports psychology consultant at Temple University in Philadelphia.

Image Isn't Everything

If you're dissatisfied with the way your body looks, take comfort in the fact that you're not alone. A survey of 296 physically active women by the Melpomene Institute for Women's Health Research in St. Paul, Minnesota, revealed that 60 percent felt they were overweight to some degree when, in reality, more than half of those women's weights were within standardized weight tables. And in another study cited by the institute, 63 percent of women overestimated their body sizes.

Society has ingrained in us the message that thinner is better. "The standard of female beauty has become more narrowly defined and restricted, making it impossible to be thin enough or fit enough," says Judy Mahle Lutter, founder and president of the Melpomene Institute. "Today, even some magazines devoted to sports activities use models who look as if they were on 800-calorie-a-day diets. In effect, the finish line keeps moving farther and farther back, ensuring that most of us will never attain the 'ideal.' "

This ever-present media standard is dangerously unhealthy, agrees Dr. Oglesby. "If you constantly compare yourself with it, you'll lose confidence. Unfortunately, the majority of women are dissatisfied with their bodies, even when they shouldn't be."

The Self-Esteem Edge

If you judge yourself solely on your appearance, you run the risk of thinking self-defeating and paralyzing thoughts. "Some women put their lives on hold," explains Nancy Clark, R.D., a nutrition counselor at SportsMedicine Brookline, an athletic injury clinic in the Boston area. "They say, 'I'm not going to put on a bathing suit and go to the beach to swim because I haven't lost ten pounds yet' or 'I'm not going to get on that bicycle and ride around so that everyone can see my tush hanging over the seat.' "

Others get sidelined by temporary fitness setbacks. Anything from a busy schedule to sickness can start a negative thought cycle going and prevent a woman from getting back into exercising. Explains Lutter, "She may think 'I used to be in shape, but now I've gained weight and I'm flabby. I feel sluggish, so I know I won't run as fast as I used to. Therefore, I don't want to put myself back out there. It will be too discouraging to have to face how much I've slipped.' "

> **S**OME WOMEN SAY, "**I**'M NOT GOING TO GET ON THAT BICYCLE AND RIDE AROUND SO THAT EVERYONE CAN SEE MY TUSH HANGING OVER THE SEAT."

Less obvious feelings of negativism can also hamper

Ten Steps to a Better Body Image

Use these simple tactics to improve your image of yourself, tune in to your body's abilities and, in turn, better your athletic performance.

1. Learn to think positively. To replace all of the self-defeating thoughts you can have in a day with positive ones, try this trick from Marjorie Snyder, Ph.D., associate director of the Women's Sports Foundation in New York City: Fill your right pocket with paper clips. Every time you think a negative thought about your body, shift a clip to your left pocket and immediately replace the thought with a positive one. Stop when you can keep all of your paper clips in the "good thought" pocket.

2. Stand tall. Straightening your stance can make you feel confident and strong. Try this posture alignment technique: Stand with your feet hip-width apart. Imagine a plumb line running through your body so that your ears, shoulders, hips, knees and ankles are all in vertical alignment. Look straight ahead, relax your shoulders and soften your knees. Feel energy flow through your body.

3. Practice deep breathing. It will teach you how to draw on your inner strength. Sit with your eyes closed. Hunch your shoulders forward; notice how difficult it is to breathe. Then sit tall and take deep, long breaths. Inhale through your nose, feeling your lungs and chest expand. Conjure up positive thoughts as you inhale. Exhale slowly, expelling any negative energy. Continue until you feel relaxed and refreshed.

your performance. For example, some women allow negativism to drain away the mental energy they need to excel. "If instead of focusing on the task at hand—say, playing a good match of tennis—you're comparing your thighs with those of the woman across the court, you won't have the

4. Put your mind into your workout. Exercises that contain meditative elements, such as tai chi and yoga, help put your mind in touch with your body, which can heighten self-awareness and self-esteem.

5. Lift weights. Weight training will strengthen and straighten you, put you in touch with your body's definition and make you feel confident in your muscles and their abilities.

6. Like what you play. When you really enjoy a particular exercise, you're more likely to stick with it and to be encouraged to try more demanding activities. But go hardcore before you're ready, and you could become frustrated and give up.

7. Use a marathon mentality. Runners tempted to quit at the 18-mile mark just focus on the next leg swing. Likewise with any fitness goal: Take it one step at a time.

8. Make a progress log. Track your daily achievements, focusing your entries on how your body is performing rather than on how it looks. For example, don't write "I lost two pounds this week." Instead, write "I ran one mile today, and I feel great."

9. See yourself achieve. If you actually visualize yourself enjoying an activity and succeeding at it, you're much more likely to do it. Athletes use this method to "see" their way around a racecourse before running it.

10. Nourish yourself. Sports nutritionists recommend three well-balanced meals a day (plus a snack). That means high-carb, low-fat foods and a nod to protein and calcium, too.

mental edge you need to play at your best," says Lutter.

Others punish their bodies with exercise, doing advanced, high-impact step classes before they're ready, driving themselves to exhaustion on rowing machines or running too far and too fast in an effort to shed those "last ten pounds." These fitness frenzies are counterproductive because they perpetuate the attitude of "I'm not good enough," says Marjorie Snyder, Ph.D., associate director of the Women's Sports Foundation in New York City. At the very least, they may leave women discouraged, feeling that they can never work out hard enough or well enough, leading them to abandon their workouts. In the worst cases, women are setting themselves up for injuries—shinsplints, muscle pulls, exhaustion and dehydration. "Approaching fitness at too difficult a level will discourage you. As a result, you're less likely to see positive results in your performance and to stay involved in the activity," says Dr. Snyder.

Some athletes eat improperly. "They get so hung up on calories and losing weight that they forget food is fuel and food is health," says Clark, who sees elite athletes in her nutrition clinic lacking energy, feeling dizzy and wondering why they're performing poorly. "I give these women permission to eat again, to nourish their bodies." Her goal is to get her clients to think about being fit, healthy and happy with their bodies.

The Perfectionist Trap

This negative mind-set can strike even competitive athletes, the women the rest of us look to as having perfect physiques. "I work with a lot of athletes who are in top shape and still find fault with their bodies," says Dr. Oglesby.

"Women who are involved in competitive sports tend to be more critical of their own fluctuations in weight than women who are not as active," adds Lutter. "They see themselves next to other women of similar age and athletic ability. They often feel they don't measure up."

Joanne Pomodoro of Boston has been plagued by a bad

body image since her high school days. "I was miserable," says Pomodoro, a top-ranked player in the women's age 40–plus U.S. Racquetball Division. Because of large breasts and a tiny, muscular frame (she is five feet one inch), she always felt she was overweight. Over the years, she battled roller-coaster weight gains and losses and obsessive running, abandoning her social life to jog up to ten miles a day. "I thought the more I ran, the thinner I would get," Pomodoro reflects. "At one point, I was existing on a diet of 500 calories a day."

Because of her poor eating habits, she began having dizzy spells and heart palpitations. "I was training very hard and eating barely anything. I started to lose weight rapidly, and I was feeling tired, grumpy and depressed. I wondered why I couldn't hit the ball quicker. I thought it was because I was a lousy athlete," she says.

Finally, Pomodoro was hospitalized with an eating disorder. Today, after counseling from sports therapists and nutritionists, she has learned to eat properly and like her body, muscles and all. "I finally realized," says Pomodoro, "that even though I don't look like a ballerina, I am strong and athletic. And I do have great legs. They're really fit."

"We tend to fall into the perfectionist trap that leads us to think there is only one right way to look," says Dr. Snyder. "But all you have to do is look around at the variety of female athletes to realize that's not true. They come in all heights, weights and sizes, and they're all in terrific shape." Instead of focusing on what your body looks like, Dr. Snyder suggests, shift your focus to what your body can do.

> **E**VEN THOUGH I DON'T LOOK LIKE A BALLERINA, I AM STRONG AND ATHLETIC. AND I DO HAVE GREAT LEGS. THEY'RE REALLY FIT.

—*Cheryl Sacra*

Beauty from the Inside Out

There's a new breed of therapist who will help you confront your self-image problems—and do something about them.

Perfectionism is tyranny. We feel so much social pressure to be perfect—perfectly coiffed, sculpted and smooth; perfect mothers, career women and mates—that many of us have distorted perceptions of what we look like or how we should look. No matter how we try, we don't measure up to those two implacable standards: young and thin.

But there has been a backlash against this self-loathing. A new breed of psychologists and therapists who treat self-image disorders are helping women to live more realistically with how they look. Acceptance is the key principle behind many of the treatments, which use behavior modification to realign out-of-focus self-awareness, whether it is relatively minor ("I hate my nose") or physically damaging (bulimia and anorexia).

Although women are still obsessed with "perfection"—compulsive exercise and weight training, chronic dieting, cosmetic surgery (up by 80 percent since 1988), makeup bingeing—many are trying to break these addictions. "Everybody has a right to go to a coach," says Janet L. Wolfe, Ph.D., executive director of the Institute for Rational-Emotive Therapy in New York City. "There are personal trainers, and there are emotional personal trainers—if you're willing to put in the time working on your psyche."

These specialists treat mostly women; female therapy patients outnumber males by two to one. The *Diagnostic and Statistical Manual of Mental Disorders* calls the syndrome body dysmorphic disorder, more commonly known as the imagined ugliness disorder. (Most men, according to one study, distort their perceptions but in more positive, self-exalting ways.) Many of the patients are not necessarily anorexic or bulimic.

HAS YOUR
SELF-CONSCIOUSNESS GROWN
INTO SELF-HATE?

More commonly, their self-image problems seem to be personal eccentricities. They may love to swim but haven't been to the beach in 15 years because they think they're too fat to wear bathing suits. Maybe they're five feet two inches but insist on purchasing tall-size panty hose that stretch halfway around the room because they think their legs are too big. Just maybe, however, these seemingly minor quirks are pathological.

But how do you know?

"To measure the seriousness of a self-image disorder," says psychologist Rita Freedman, Ph.D., author of *Bodylove: Feeling Good about Your Looks and Yourself*, "is to determine how disruptive the condition is to your life." Is your self-consciousness debilitating, and has it grown into self-hate? Some of the symptoms: You can't go into an airport or a hotel lobby for fear of being seen; it takes you hours to get dressed in the morning; you spend a large proportion of each day exercising (unless you're a professional athlete) and feel extremely anxious if you miss a day; you can't make love with the lights on or during the daytime; or you get turned off sexually when you see yourself naked in a mirror. The case histories of women with pathological self-image disorders, says Dr. Freedman, "often reveal inclinations toward obsessive-compulsive or manic-depressive disorders."

Focusing on the Moment

Like most self-image therapists, Dr. Freedman centers her treatment, at least initially, on the present rather than the deep past. Using behavior modification, or what she calls cognitive behavioral techniques, Dr. Freedman asks her patients what they're doing or thinking just before they feel troubled. She starts with the most dysfunctional behavior and works out a plan to modify it and to encourage them. One of her patients, for example, is so self-conscious about her hair that she washes it 15 times a day, yet she is never satisfied that it is clean or shiny enough. Another is mirror-obsessed. In treatment, Dr. Freedman will suggest that the shampoo fanatic wash her hair 5 times instead of 15. The mirror gazer might be asked to count how many times she looks at her reflection every day.

In confronting a body image problem, a woman must face up to it, but without losing her sense of proportion. For severe cases, as well as for those patients who experience occasional self-image conflicts, Dr. Wolfe frequently draws pie charts. She instructs the patients to label the slices: body size and shape, friendship skills, work competence, artistic abilities. This helps show them that they hurt only themselves when they take one slice of the pie—friendship skills, for example—and define their entire worth by it. For Dr. Wolfe, this means "disputing images that have become norms in culture," or what she calls sex role–related "shoulds." (If you are wondering about your own behavior in this area, take Dr. Wolfe's quiz in "How's Your Self-Image?" on page 234.)

How Acceptance Plays a Role

Striving to look good is all right, as long as you are setting your ultimate standard realistically. "Driving, hounding, insulting or abusing yourself is not good," Dr. Wolfe says. She helps women see that "I'm fat, therefore I'm no good" is not fact—it's a belief. "Where is it written that you can't look and feel good with a certain amount of body fat?" she asks.

At least one woman, Sally E. Smith, thinks you can. Smith is the executive director of the National Association to Advance Fat Acceptance, an organization devoted to ending discrimination based on body size. "Sizism," she says, "is one of the last safe prejudices. People who wouldn't dream of making sexist, racist or homophobic comments have no problem making fat jokes."

In a culture bent on perfection, the overriding message is that your character is weak if you can't control your weight. Because being fat is associated with being lazy, stupid and sloppy, overweight is taken to mean that you're underdisciplined and overindulgent. According to Smith, however, the latest evidence suggests that restrictive diets don't work. According to a Weight-Loss Technology Assessment conference sponsored by the National Institutes of Health in Bethesda, Maryland, 95 percent of dieters fail diets and

> SIZISM IS ONE OF THE LAST SAFE PREJUDICES. PEOPLE WHO WOULDN'T DREAM OF MAKING SEXIST, RACIST OR HOMOPHOBIC COMMENTS HAVE NO PROBLEM MAKING FAT JOKES.

(continued on page 236)

How's Your Self-Image?

Most women suffer from self-image disorders to some degree, according to Janet L. Wolfe, Ph.D., executive director of the Institute for Rational-Emotive Therapy in New York City. Dr. Wolfe put together this questionnaire to help you assess your image of yourself.

1. Do you avoid looking in the mirror or weighing yourself for fear of what you'll see?

2. When you look in the mirror, do you zero in on your negative features?

3. Do you spend a large portion of your time focused on how you look—for example, buying clothes and cosmetics or reading material on diets?

4. Do you tend to rate much of your worth as a person on the basis of how you look?

5. Are you frequently depressed about your appearance?

6. Do you believe that you cannot be happy until you lose weight?

7. Do you postpone things you would like to do because of your appearance?

8. Do you spend a lot of time envying the way others look and comparing yourself negatively with them?

9. Is the weight goal you've set for yourself not realistic for your genetic background?

10. Do you exercise more than eight hours a week in order to lose or maintain your weight?

11. Have you ever employed purging (through vomiting or laxatives) to offset binge eating?

12. Do you regularly ask for reassurance about the way you look and then are skeptical when people respond affirmatively?

13. Do you avoid body-pleasuring activities (massages,

sex) because you believe you don't deserve them?

14. Do you long to look like a woman with Barbie-doll proportions?

If you answered yes to one to three of these questions, you have a mild to moderate problem in physical self-acceptance, says Dr. Wolfe; to four to eight questions, your lack of self-acceptance is a serious problem; to more than eight of these questions, you have a severe problem with your self-image. You should see a cognitive behavior therapist, preferably one who helps people with problems of depression and self-acceptance.

Dr. Wolfe suggests trying the following exercises to increase self-acceptance.

- Find women with imperfect bodies who seem content with themselves. Ask them questions about how their lives differ before and after acceptance.
- Indulge in body-pleasing experiences (massages, shopping for new clothes).
- Every time you have a negative thought about your body, follow it up with a positive one.
- Complete this sentence: "Because of my looks, I can not. . . " Then make a counterargument against the statement.
- Write yourself a love letter, including all of the wonderful things that make you unique and special.

If, after repeating these exercises, you begin to feel more at peace with your body, you are on the path to self-acceptance, Dr. Wolfe says. If not, chances are you need a professional to help you get rid of some of your deeply entrenched negative perceptions.

gain the weight back. The focus, Smith feels, should be less on dieting and more on positive self-image.

According to a study by Debbie Then, Ph.D., a Stanford, California, psychologist, 85 percent of American women are afflicted with body image disorders. The U.S. Department of Health and Human Services says that 47 percent of normal-weight women want to be thinner and that 16 percent of those who are already considered underweight want to be even thinner than they are.

The trend also afflicts the next generation. As many as 80 percent of 10- and 11-year-old girls don't eat normally because they want to be thin, according to Frances Berg, editor of the *Healthy Weight Journal.* "If you're a little girl watching your mother, one of the things you're bound to learn is to watch your weight all of the time," explains Barbara Altman Bruno, Ph.D., a clinical social worker in the New York City area. "We're raised to be at war with our outer selves."

Rita Hovakimian has seen her share of women at war with their bodies. Hovakimian used to be a top personal trainer in San Francisco with a specialty in exercise physiology. She kept running up against the same obstacles. "It didn't matter what kind of fantastic body a woman had, how hard she worked out, how she had gotten her fat percentage down—she was never satisfied."

So Hovakimian left physical workouts behind to concentrate on mental strengthening. She created the Body Esteem Workshop, a two-day course aimed at improving self-image. She now travels around the country lecturing and running workshops for working women ages 20 to 60. She uses mirror exercises, small group discussions and journal writing to help women create their beauty images from the inside out.

As host of *Love Phones*, a call-in radio show, clinical psychologist and sex therapist Judy Kuriansky, Ph.D., says she often hears from young women who feel that they're not pretty enough or that their breasts are too small or too big. They walk around with feelings of inadequacy that inhibit their self-esteem and sexuality. She attributes those feelings, at least in part, to "a society that says you have to have luscious lips like Kim Basinger or a body like Kathy Ireland." But there's good news, she adds. Research has shown that female sexual response improves when women develop positive attitudes toward their bodies and raise their overall self-esteem.

Trust Mother Nature

Even the cosmetics industry is addressing issues that are more than skin deep. Famous slogans from the 1980s, such as "Don't hate me because I'm beautiful" (with its implied "and you're not"), have evolved into more accepting messages, such as Clinique's "Beauty isn't about looking young." Smaller cosmetics companies such as Trucco have introduced natural-looking colors and textures be-cause they understand that although women want to look good, comfort is a priority as well.

ON BAD DAYS, MAYBE EVEN **CINDY CRAWFORD** HAS **TROUBLE.**

When designer Norma Kamali created her signature beauty line, she decided to skip foundation, eye shadow and black mascara and focus on the skin. Her cosmetics reflect a commitment to minimalism; the point is not to mask the face but to reveal it. "Everybody is going to have something she doesn't like about her skin," says Kamali. "For instance, I have dark circles around my eyes. But hey, this is me. A perfect, spackled face is not what I'm about. I want to look good, but I also want to look natural."

The point is to trust Mother Nature. "We're all looking

for ways to become more powerful," says Dr. Freedman. In the past, she explains, "the one power women had was physical attractiveness." But as more women break through the mystique of physical perfectionism and reach a clear sense of the total self, image problems shouldn't damage the psyche to quite the same degree.

The next time your thighs stand in the way of your happiness, think of Eleanor Roosevelt, a woman of great accomplishment. When asked whether she had any regrets about her life, Roosevelt replied, "Just one. I wish I'd been prettier."

So everyone but goddesses feels the same way—and on bad days, maybe even Cindy Crawford has trouble. The real point is to never let it stop you.

—Rona Berg with Kate Staples

Part IX
Low-Fat, No-Fuss Feasts

A Salmon Sampler

At less than ten grams of fat per serving, salmon earns a respectable spot on a dieter's menu.

Slashing through the cold, dark streams of Scotland, surging up the coast of Oregon and Washington, gliding majestically through the waters of Alaska—sleek, silvery salmon never fail to excite fishermen. And whether set out poached and garnished as the decorative center of attention at a banquet table, laden smoked and savory onto a bagel or barbecued and striped from the grill, the beautiful peachy-pink flesh of salmon never fails to excite the most discriminating of eaters.

Salmon, our most adaptable, most kingly of fish, is surging in popularity these days, not only for its versatility and wonderful taste but also for its wondrous nutritional benefits.

At one time, an expensive cut of red meat was the dish of choice at a party banquet table. These days, top caterers are more apt to turn to salmon as their top-of-the-line entrée recommendation, and savvy party givers are apt to agree with them.

The wonderful new thing about salmon, however,

is that it is no longer a dish fit just for kings or expense-account diners. With salmon being farmed in greater quantities than ever, the price for this exquisite fish and the quality available are better than at any time in history.

Keep Salmon Simple

The extraordinary thing about salmon is that it remains unique—distinctively itself, no matter how it's cooked. Salmon done up Cajun, Chinese or Catalan always seems to taste of salmon alone rather than of its attempted style. Other fish may disappear into generic "fishiness" under a deluge of frying or saucing, but salmon always stands up for itself.

The reasons that we should also stand up for salmon are legion. Salmon is, without a doubt, the most palatable and delicate of all of the fish that are considered oily. Nutritionists are the first to point out that the oily fish contain omega-3 fatty acids, one of the good kinds of fat. Omega-3 fatty acids are associated with reduced heart attack and stroke and with less risk of inflammatory diseases such as rheumatoid arthritis.

Salmon, like all fish, is super-low in artery-clogging saturated fat. Plus it stocks some vitamin A, vitamin D, B vitamins and potassium. For an extra dose of calcium, crumble the bones in canned salmon and eat them, too.

Ice It

Purchase only as much fresh salmon as you want to cook in the next 24 hours. Put it on a bed of ice in a flat container in the coldest part of the refrigerator as soon as possible after its purchase. Cover it with wax paper. If you're lucky enough to have a fisherman in the family, freshly caught salmon can be frozen in a deep-freeze chest—but never in the freezer section of your refrigerator. (It's not cold enough to freeze the fish quickly.) Thaw frozen salmon for no more than 30 minutes at room temperature. It should be partially defrosted but still firm.

The Ten-Minute Rule

Because salmon is at its best when it's cooked by a delicate hand, be particularly conscious of cooking times and simplicity of preparation. Measure salmon fillets and steaks at their thickest points, then apply the ten-minute rule in all cooking situations, from poaching to baking to broiling: For each inch of thickness, allow ten minutes' cooking time. Baste the fish with water once or twice if you're broiling or baking.

These days, trendy restaurants like to leave salmon slightly rare in the middle, sometimes presenting very raw portions of fish when the diner cuts into the center. Better that the fish should flake through its thickest point for optimum eating reliability. So cook the flesh until it's opaque, then gently test the fish by inserting a fork or knifepoint at the thickest section of the fish, gently pulling the flesh aside. Look for flaking with no raw center for the healthiest and most tasteful dining.

If you are cooking the fish in a sauce preparation or wrapping it in foil with a stuffing in the cavity, add an extra five minutes to the cooking time.

For tasty and innovative ways to prepare and serve this majestic fish, see the following recipes.

Salmon Accompaniments

Whether you choose to broil a salmon steak or poach a tail section, whether you make salmon cakes or salmon burgers from canned fish, there are certain accompaniments that seem to attend salmon with special grace.

Yes, salmon goes well with white, brown or wild rice. But don't forget that staple Russian dish *kulebiaka*, in which salmon is baked, along with mushrooms and a garnish of hard-cooked eggs, on a bed of cracked bulgur wheat or buckwheat kasha. Salmon can stand up to these healthy grains with no loss of face.

There is no prettier salmon presentation than a blue and white plate, a serving of pink fish and a green vegetable. A quick sauté of spinach and garlic, fresh steamed asparagus or broccoli will do nicely. But for wonderful counterpoint delicacy, try the crunch of cucumbers. Sliced cucumbers become a wonderful, crisp salad when simply dressed with yogurt, lemons and chopped fresh dill. Cooked cucumbers are wonderful as well: Peel and carve them into seedless ovals, then simply parboil them until crisp-tender and dress them with fresh dill and a few drops of olive oil.

One of the freshest ways to present salmon is in the *lomi lomi* style of Hawaii. Cube cooked or lightly smoked salmon, then mix it with equal amounts of cubed tomatoes, mild red onions and minced parsley. Dress with lemon juice and a few drops of olive oil, then mound on a bed of lettuce leaves.

CRUSTED SALMON HASH

Per serving: 341 calories, 9.1 g. fat (24% of calories), 1.4 g. dietary fiber, 23.2 g. protein, 40.7 g. carbohydrates, 47 milligrams cholesterol, 416 mg. sodium. Also a very good source of B vitamins, vitamin C, potassium and iron.

Serves 4

> 4 **medium potatoes, peeled and cut into ½″ cubes**
> ¾ **pound skinless, boneless fresh salmon, cut into ½″ cubes**
> 1 **medium white onion, chopped**
> 2 **cloves garlic, minced**
> 1 **tender stalk celery, sliced**
> 2 **sweet yellow or orange peppers, minced**
> 3 **tablespoons minced parsley**
> 1 **teaspoon fresh or dried savory**
> ¼ **teaspoon cayenne pepper**
> **Freshly ground black pepper**
> 1 **tablespoon olive oil**
> ½ **cup nonfat sour cream**
> **Lemon wedges**
> **Salsa**

1. In a vegetable steamer, steam the potatoes until fork-tender, about 6 to 8 minutes. When the potatoes are cooked, remove from the steamer and place the salmon in the steamer basket. Steam until the fish turns uniformly pale, about 3 to 4 minutes.

2. Meanwhile, coat a 10″ no-stick frying pan with cooking spray. Heat over medium heat and add the onions, garlic, celery, half of the yellow or orange peppers (reserving the remaining half for garnish) and ¼ cup water. Cook, covered, until the onions are tender and the water has evaporated. Add the potatoes to the onion mixture and cook together over medium heat. Using a spatula, turn over the mass frequently, allowing a light crust to form.

3. Turn out the potatoes into a large bowl. Add the salmon, parsley, savory, cayenne pepper and black pepper

to taste. Turn the mass gently to mix, but do not allow the salmon to break apart too much.

4. Clean the frying pan and heat the oil. Pack the hash mixture into the frying pan and press firmly. Cover and cook over medium-low heat for 2 minutes. Remove the cover; press and compact the mixture again. Cover and cook for 2 more minutes. Uncover and again firm the mixture with the back of a fork or spatula. Continue cooking, uncovered, until a dense golden crust has formed and the hash cake slips easily in the pan when shaken.

5. Reverse the hash cake onto a serving platter and serve at once, topped with a scoop of the remaining yellow or orange peppers and a dollop of nonfat sour cream. Accompany with a lemon wedge and a side of salsa.

BAKED SALMON CAKES WITH CUCUMBER SLAW

Per serving: 489 calories, 10.1 g. fat (19% of calories), 6.2 g. dietary fiber, 34.4 g. protein, 67.8 g. carbohydrates, 65 mg. cholesterol, 559 mg. sodium. Also a very good source of B vitamins, vitamins A and C, potassium, calcium, iron and magnesium.

Serves 4

> **2 cucumbers, peeled, halved lengthwise and seeded**
> **1 pound skinless, boneless cooked salmon, cut into 1″ chunks**
> **2 egg whites**
> **1 cup finely crushed unsalted saltines**
> **2 tablespoons minced onions**
> **1 tablespoon Dijon mustard**
> **2 teaspoons minced garlic**
> **1 teaspoon lemon rind**
> **1 teaspoon Old Bay seasoning**
> **¼ teaspoon cayenne pepper**
> **Freshly ground black pepper**
> **1 teaspoon olive oil**
> **⅔ cup low-fat plain yogurt**
> **1 teaspoon minced fresh dill**
> **Juice of ½ lemon**
> **4 hamburger rolls**
> **Lemon wedges**
> **Oven-roasted root vegetables**

1. Shred the cucumbers through the medium-large blade of a grater into a medium bowl and refrigerate.

2. Place the salmon and egg whites in the bowl of a food processor and puree. Scrape down the sides of the bowl, then stir in ¾ cup saltines and the onions, mustard, garlic, lemon rind, seasoning, cayenne pepper and black pepper to taste. Cover the mixture and refrigerate for 30 minutes.

3. Place aluminum foil on a baking sheet. Shape the chilled salmon mixture into four patties and place on the

foil. Pat the remaining ¼ cup saltines over the tops of the salmon patties. Drizzle the oil over each top.

4. Cover the patties with aluminum foil and bake for 20 minutes. Then remove the foil and broil briefly until the saltine crumbs are golden brown.

5. While the salmon cakes are baking, squeeze all of the moisture out of the cucumbers. Stir in the yogurt, dill and lemon juice. Serve the salmon cakes on hamburger rolls (or bread), like fish sandwiches, with the lemon wedges and cucumber slaw on the side. Oven-roasted or grilled root vegetables complete the scene for this nautical nosh.

Warm Salmon Salad with Gazpacho Dressing

Per serving: 640 calories, 17 g. fat (24% of calories), 7.4 g. dietary fiber, 39.1 g. protein, 82.3 g. carbohydrates, 62.7 mg. cholesterol, 747 mg. sodium. Also a very good source of B vitamins, vitamins A and C, potassium, calcium, magnesium and iron.

Serves 4

Salad

  8 large romaine lettuce leaves
  8 cups assorted young, tender greens (spinach, frisée, mâche, watercress)
  4 5-ounce salmon steaks (1¼″ thick)
 ½ cup flour
  2 teaspoons olive oil

Dressing

  1 small red onion, diced
  2 teaspoons olive oil
 ⅓ cup low-sodium tomato juice
  1 small red bell pepper, seeded and diced
  3 tablespoons balsamic or red-wine vinegar
  1 large clove garlic, pressed
     Pinch cayenne pepper
     Freshly ground black pepper
  1 small avocado, cubed (optional)
 12 cherry tomatoes, halved
  1 1-pound French baguette

1. *To make the salad:* Arrange two of the romaine lettuce leaves on each of four dinner plates. Arrange a scattering of the greens around each plate, leaving the plate centers bare for the salad. Set aside in the refrigerator.

2. Remove the center backbone of each salmon steak and neatly cut each steak in two, leaving on the skin. Fit the two steak halves together, thick end to thin end, with their centers touching. Tie together each pair of steaks with string.

3. Spread the flour on a plate and dip the steaks in it to coat.

4. Heat the oil in a 10″ no-stick frying pan. Re-dip each steak in the flour to ensure a heavy coating. Fry the steaks on one side over medium heat for about 3 minutes, or until a golden crust forms. Lower the heat and fry the steaks on the other side for another 4 to 5 minutes.

5. Cut off the string and remove the skin from each steak. Place one steak in the center of each plate of greens.

6. *To make the dressing:* Place the onions, oil and tomato juice in a clean frying pan. Heat to simmer and let the onions wilt briefly. Turn off the heat and mix in the red peppers, vinegar, garlic, cayenne pepper and black pepper. Give the pan a few shakes to mix the ingredients, then spoon the dressing over each steak and onto the greens. Scatter the avocados (if using) and tomatoes on each plate. Serve with lots of crusty chunks of the French baguette.

ORIENTAL SALMON WITH BLACK BEANS AND HERBS

Per serving: 467 calories, 9.2 g. fat (18% of calories), 3.8 g. dietary fiber, 30.7 g. protein, 63.3 g. carbohydrates, 62.7 mg. cholesterol, 338 mg. sodium. Also a very good source of B vitamins, vitamin C, potassium, magnesium and iron.

Serves 4

> 1 **pound center-cut salmon fillet, boned and well-chilled**
> 1 **scallion, trimmed**
> 1 **medium tomato**
> 2 **tablespoons fermented black beans**
> ⅓ **cup clam juice**
> 1 **tablespoon light soy sauce**
> 1 **tablespoon rice or white-wine vinegar**
> 1 **teaspoon sesame oil**
> **Handful of mixed fresh Italian parsley and cilantro**
> 4 **cups cooked rice**
> **Steamed broccoli rabe**

1. Cut the salmon into ⅓″-thick horizontal slices (about 12). Place the slices between two sheets of plastic wrap and flatten to ⅛″ with a meat pounder. Line a baking sheet with aluminum foil and lightly oil the foil. Place the flattened slices on the foil, cover and refrigerate until needed.

2. Cut the scallion into thin slices and separate into rings. Cut the tomato in half across the middle and gently squeeze out all of the seeds and juice. Cut the remaining flesh into ¼″ cubes.

3. Place the beans in a sieve and rinse under hot water to remove any salt. Blot dry. Reserve the scallions, tomatoes and beans for garnish.

4. Mix the clam juice, soy sauce, vinegar and oil. Heat almost to a simmer. Heat a broiler. Brush the salmon with half of the clam-juice mixture. Broil the salmon on one side only for 1 minute. Immediately transfer to four warm plates,

The Key to Perfect Salmon

When shopping for fresh salmon, here are some tips for selecting the freshest fish.

- Use your nose, eyes and fingers when you select your purchase. Bring fish up to your nose and sniff for a slightly salty, fresh seaweed odor, as opposed to a strong, oily odor.
- Feel the flesh of the fish. There should be a firm, slightly elastic quality, a certain resistance to the flesh. If you are buying a whole fish or a side, run your finger over the scales. They should stick tightly to the salmon's skin. Press the fish with your finger; if it leaves an indentation, it's probably old fish. Cut fillets and steaks should feel firm, not watery or flaccid.
- If you don't want to deal with pinbones, purchase tail sections of salmon, which are always boneless. (The best way to remove pinbones from salmon, by the way, is with a pair of pliers.)
- To judge the quality of canned salmon, stand the can upright at room temperature for a night. Open the can, gently press on the fish and spoon off some of the oil that comes to the surface. The more oil and the richer its color, the better the quality of the fish. The fish should also feel firm and be an attractive pink color.

scatter the plates with the reserved scallions, tomatoes and beans and the parsley and cilantro and drizzle with the remaining clam-juice mixture. Serve with the rice and broccoli rabe.

—Judith Olney with Barb Fritz and the Rodale Test Kitchen

Green Giants

With so few calories, simply prepared garden greens are compatible with anyone's weight-loss plans.

You can never get enough glorious greens, no matter how—or even if—you cook them. That's because the more you eat of them, the better off you are. Collectively, greens are the one food you can love that loves you right back. Chicory, Swiss chard, kale, dandelion, radicchio—the list goes on and on.

To some people, these may seem like part of a foreign language primer. But don't let strange-sounding names put you off. We realize that even though you know deep down these curious vegetables are great for you, they may be somewhat intimidating at first.

So we'll take it slowly and introduce you to a few of these green giants, glossary-style, and show you that there's a whole spectrum of delicious green tastes and good-for-you fare out there, just waiting to be explored.

All of the greens in the glossary are readily available in most supermarkets; just take a stroll down the emerald aisle. You'll find that these greens are great in salads, soups and stews. Or simply cook them alone, then add a splash of olive oil or citrus juice and a sprinkle of Parmesan or chopped nuts. Or try the recipes beginning on page 259 for other heart-healthy suggestions.

Beet greens. These are actually the green tops of the beet root vegetable and may be sold attached to full-size beets or in bunches by themselves. The long-stemmed, green or greenish red leaves are significantly more nutritious than their ruby red roots. Beet greens are best when young. They're available year-round; the peak season is June through October.

Nutrient profile: 1.4 milligrams beta-carotene, 45 milligrams calcium, 1.4 grams fiber and 11 milligrams vitamin C; seven calories. (These numbers, and those for the following vegetables, are based on one cup of raw greens.)

Tip: Be forewarned—beet greens tend to bleed when cooked and will impart a red color if added to soups.

Chicory greens. The greens with gusto! Also known as curly endive; pleasantly bitter-tasting. Look for narrow leaves that have curly edges and are curling at the ends. The center should be yellowish white, with darker outer leaves that are tender and crisp with no signs of wilting. Available year-round. Trendy radicchio is a red-leafed Italian chicory.

Nutrient profile: Chicory tops the green scene as an excellent source of vitamin C (43 milligrams), calcium (180 milligrams), folate (197 micrograms), magnesium (54 milligrams) and potassium (756 milligrams); 41 calories.

Tip: It's not easy being green, so use a light touch when cooking. Otherwise, you'll lose some valuable water-soluble nutrients and texture.

Dandelion greens. Bright green, jagged-edged leaves with a strong, tart flavor, dandelion greens grow both wild (in your own backyard!) and cultivated. Peak season: early spring, before plants begin to develop their infamous

Gussy Up Those Greens

You probably think that if you've tried one green, you've tried them all—they'll taste the same no matter how you cook them. *Au contraire!* It's true that most greens are interchangeable in recipes, but their characteristics vary greatly. And a lot actually hinges on how you prepare them and with what. Don't forget that creative seasoning packs greens with fantastic flavor, not fat. So turn over a new leaf and veer away from buttery, creamy sauces. Stick to gourmet seasoning mixes and follow these cooking suggestions for some groovy green grazing.

Wilting with No Fat

1. Clean the greens (see "Clean Greens Are Happy Greens" on page 256) and have them ready in a colander. Don't shake off all of the water; it helps to steam the greens and wilt them.

2. Heat a large no-stick frying pan over medium to high heat.

3. Add the wet greens (you have to begin with a mountain of greens; one pound raw equals one cup cooked) to the hot frying pan and cook, covered, over medium-high heat until the greens are wilted and bright green. This procedure takes only a few minutes. Serve with a dollop of nonfat plain yogurt mixed with horseradish and chives.

yellow flowers. At this point, the leaves become tough and bitter. Look for bright green, tender-crisp leaves with no yellowing or wilted tips.

Nutrient profile: Excellent source of beta-carotene (4.6 milligrams) and calcium (103 milligrams) and a good source of vitamin C (19 milligrams) and iron; 24 calories.

Tip: Avoid Green Beret tactics; handle greens with

Wilting with a Small Amount of Fat

Follow the steps above, but at step 2, add a small amount of olive oil to the frying pan. When the oil is hot, add some chopped garlic and sauté until golden. Add the wet greens and continue with step 3. Serve over pasta.

Braising

If your greens are tough and strong, take the wilting procedure one step further. After the greens are wilted in the pan, stir in a little stock or water, cover, turn down the heat to medium-low and cook a bit longer. After about 5 minutes, taste and be your own judge. As a final touch, drizzle some lemon juice or apple cider over the greens before serving.

Bonus: The gentle braising method produces a delicious "pot liquor"—the liquid in the pan. Serve with a hunk of crunchy French bread for sopping up every last drop.

Microwaving

Toss chopped fresh greens into a glass dish. Splash on some stock and cover with vented plastic wrap. Microwave on high until just tender, about two minutes for two cups of greens. Allow to stand for two minutes, then drain. Add to casseroles, stir-fries and rice dishes, or serve simply and elegantly with a sprinkling of Parmesan or feta cheese and chopped nuts.

tender loving care. Cuts and bruises invite decay.

Kale. Thick, handsomely ruffled, grayish blue to green, kale is perhaps the most misunderstood green. It's often called upon to act as window dressing at salad bars, probably because it stays fresh for so long when perched on a bed of crushed ice. Green with envy, kale longs to be part of the mix. Boasting a mild cabbage flavor, it's as versatile

Clean Greens Are Happy Greens

• Clean your greens as soon as you whisk them home from the market, especially if they're wet. Wet leaves tend to rot easily. Discard the tatty, imperfect leaves. Break apart whole heads and remove thick stems, such as those on spinach.

• Fill your sink or a large bowl with cold water. Add the leaves and swish them around with your hands to dislodge dirt and grit. But don't soak: Soaking dissolves some of the valuable nutrients. Change the water once or twice if the leaves are especially dirty. Transfer to a colander and give the leaves a final cold-water rinse.

• If you are cooking the greens immediately, give them a slight shake, but allow some water droplets to remain for more even cooking.

• If you plan to store your greens, dry well between paper or cotton towels, or use a salad spinner.

• Store in plastic bags that have been perforated for air circulation. Close securely, refrigerate and use within three to four days.

as spinach and—guess what?—it is meant to be eaten! Avoid yellowed leaves. Kale is available year-round; its season peaks January through April.

Nutrient profile: A member of the crucifer family. High in vitamin C (80 milligrams), potassium (299 milligrams), beta-carotene (3.58 milligrams) and calcium (90 milligrams); 33 calories.

Tip: With kale, looks are everything. Choose leaves with good green color and a crisp, moist, clean, cold appearance. And remember, the darker green the leaf, the higher the nutritional food value.

Mustard greens. Thinner and softer in texture than most varieties of greens, with a tempting, tangy mustard flavor. Look for crisp, young leaves with a bright green color. Avoid yellowed, flabby or pitted leaves, leaves with mustard seeds attached (a sign of overmaturity) and thick, fibrous stems. Peak season: December through early March.

Nutrient profile: A member of the crucifer family. Good source of vitamin C (39 milligrams), folate (105 micrograms) and calcium (58 milligrams); only 15 calories!

Tip: Give the green light to quantity—cook enough. Volume reduces drastically during cooking. One pound raw equals one cup cooked.

Spinach. Musky flavor with a coarse texture. Look for fresh, crisp, dark green outer leaves that are free from dirt and debris. Inner leaves will be pale, crinkled and very tender. Wimpy, wilted, limp or brownish leaves have lost vitamin C. Available year-round. Spinach is superb cooked or raw. Lightly steamed, fresh spinach has excellent flavor and texture. Fresh, perky raw spinach shines in a salad alone but is also very compatible with other greens. Try it with fruits such as strawberries or mandarin oranges, a few red onion slices and a splash of olive oil. Outstanding!

Nutrient profile: 109 micrograms of folate (27 percent of the Daily Value), 44 milligrams of magnesium, 312 milligrams of potassium and 16 milligrams of vitamin C; only 14 calories.

Tip: Spinach has stamina. When stored at 34° to 36°F with a relative humidity of 90 to 95 percent, spinach holds on to its green genes for at least 10 to 14 days.

Swiss chard. Fleshy, silvery, celery stalk–like stems with broad, crisp, crinkly green leaves. The sturdy stems are often used like celery or asparagus in cooking. Swiss chard leaves, with their sweet, earthy taste and slightly bitter undertones, can be cooked like any other green. Peak season: April through November.

Nutrient profile: Chard boasts 11 milligrams of vitamin C and is a source of magnesium; only six calories.

Tip: Never boil chard; boiling removes the flavor. Always steam.

Turnip greens. Much like beet greens, these lean greens are savored as a vegetable. Slightly sweet when young and tender, turnip greens become tough and strong-flavored with age. Buy only fresh, crisp, even-colored green turnip tops; avoid those that are wilted or off-color. Prepare like spinach. Peak season: October through February.

Nutrient profile: Another star, with only 15 calories per cup; 105 milligrams calcium, 107 micrograms folate, 33 milligrams vitamin C and 2.5 milligrams beta-carotene.

Tip: Don't store greens in the same refrigerator drawer as you do ethylene-producing fruits such as apples; the greens will develop brown spots and decay rapidly.

PORTUGUESE-STYLE KALE SOUP

Per serving: 358 calories, 8.5 g. fat (21% of calories), 7.4 g. dietary fiber, 18 g. protein, 56.7 g. carbohydrates, 25 mg. cholesterol, 284 mg. sodium. Also a very good source of vitamins A, B$_6$ and C and folate.

Serves 4

¼ **pound low-fat Italian sausage**
1 **tablespoon olive oil**
2 **medium onions, chopped (about 3 cups)**
5 **cloves garlic, minced**
6 **large boiling potatoes, cut into ½″ chunks (about 5 cups)**
1 **bay leaf**
7 **cups defatted chicken stock**
   Pinch of red-pepper flakes (optional)
1 **large bunch kale, stems removed and cut into 2″ pieces**
¼ **teaspoon black pepper**

1. Brown the sausage in a no-stick frying pan over medium heat, turning often, for about 20 minutes, or until cooked through. Remove from the heat and transfer to a cutting surface. Allow to cool slightly, then cut into ½″-thick slices.

2. Heat the oil in a medium-size heavy saucepan over medium heat. Add the onions and cook until translucent but not browned, about 10 minutes. Stir in the garlic and sauté for 1 minute. Add the potatoes, bay leaf, stock and red-pepper flakes (if using).

3. Bring the mixture to a boil, reduce the heat and simmer until the potatoes are soft, about 30 minutes. Using the back of a wooden spoon, mash the potatoes against the sides of the pot to thicken the soup. Remove the bay leaf and discard. Puree half of the soup in a blender. Return to the pot. Stir in the sausage, kale and pepper. Cook for 5 more minutes. Serve with hunks of crunchy French bread.

BITTER GREENS SALAD WITH CITRUS AND PEARS

Per serving: 313 calories, 8.1 g. fat (23% of calories), 6.3 g. dietary fiber, 9.3 g. protein, 54.2 g. carbohydrates, 0 mg. cholesterol, 369 mg. sodium. Also a very good source of vitamins A and C, folate and thiamin.

Serves 4

- 6 cups mixed young, tender greens (chicory, escarole hearts, radicchio, frisée, dandelion)
- 2 ripe sweet pears (Comice or other)
- ½ teaspoon orange rind
- 2 sweet oranges
- 1 tablespoon orange juice
- 1 tablespoon sherry vinegar
- 1½ teaspoons olive oil
- 1 French baguette (about 8 ounces), sliced into 8 pieces
- 3 tablespoons coarsely chopped walnuts, lightly toasted

1. Clean and trim the greens, discarding any tough or yellowed leaves. Wash, spin-dry and wrap them in a kitchen towel. Refrigerate the greens until ready to use.

2. Cut the pears into thin slices lengthwise. Sprinkle them with lemon juice to keep the slices from browning.

3. Scrape the orange rind from the oranges with a zester. Then using a very sharp knife, remove the peel and pith from the oranges, being sure to remove every bit of white. Slice the oranges into ¼"-thick slices.

4. To prepare the vinaigrette, mix together the orange rind, orange juice, vinegar and 1 teaspoon olive oil in a small bowl. Rub the remaining ½ teaspoon olive oil on the bread slices and lightly toast in a 350° oven, crouton-style.

5. Place the greens in a large bowl and toss with half of the vinaigrette. Divide among 4 salad plates. Arrange the pears, oranges and walnuts on top, then drizzle with the remaining vinaigrette. Top with the croutons.

CHARD AND WHITE BEAN GRATIN

Per serving: 276 calories, 7.4 g. fat (24% of calories), 2.8 g. dietary fiber, 17 g. protein, 38.4 g. carbohydrates, 9.9 mg. cholesterol, 566 mg. sodium. Also a very good source of vitamins A and C, calcium, folate and potassium.

Serves 4

    1 teaspoon olive oil
    1 teaspoon red-pepper flakes
    2 cloves garlic, minced
    2 medium bunches Swiss chard, rinsed (allowing water droplets to cling to the leaves) and cut into 2″ strips (12 cups)
    1 19-ounce can cannellini beans
    1 large tomato, chopped, or 1 cup drained and chopped canned tomatoes
    1 tablespoon chopped fresh sage or 1 teaspoon dried thyme
  ½ cup coarse, dry bread crumbs
  ½ cup freshly grated Parmesan cheese
    1 teaspoon olive oil

1. In a large sauté pan, heat the oil over medium heat and add the red-pepper flakes. Stir lightly. Add the garlic and cook until just golden. Add the chard and wilt for 3 minutes. Add the beans and heat through, about 5 minutes. Add the tomatoes and sage or thyme, stir and remove from the heat.

2. Preheat the oven to 350°. Spread the chard mixture in a 1½-quart casserole or gratin dish that has been lightly coated with no-stick cooking spray. Sprinkle with the bread crumbs and Parmesan and drizzle with the oil. Bake for 30 minutes, or until browned and bubbly.

WINTER PRIMAVERA

Per serving: 579 calories, 15.5 g. fat (24% of calories), 2.1 g. dietary fiber, 16.4 g. protein, 93.6 g. carbohydrates, 0 mg. cholesterol, 125 mg. sodium. Also a very good source of vitamin C, niacin, riboflavin, thiamin and magnesium.

Serves 4

- ¼ **cup olive oil**
- 8 **cloves garlic**
- 2 **red onions, thinly sliced**
- 2 **bunches Swiss chard or 1 head escarole, cut into 2″ strips (6–8 cups)**
- 1 **pound penne or other short, bite-size pasta**

1. Heat the oil in a large, heavy frying pan over medium heat. Add the garlic and onions. Sauté for 5 minutes. Reduce the heat to low and continue cooking, stirring often, for about 20 minutes, or until soft and glazed. Be careful not to burn. Remove the frying pan from the stove.

2. Cut the garlic into small pieces. Return the pan to medium heat and add the chard or escarole in batches, stirring to combine after each addition. Cook until the greens are wilted, about 3 minutes.

3. In the meantime, bring about 2 quarts of water to boil in a large pot. Cook the penne or other pasta according to package directions. Drain the pasta and toss gently with the wilted greens.

—Mary Nagle with Teresa Yeykal, Barb Fritz and the Rodale Test Kitchen

Low-Fat Chips 'n' Dips

America's most celebrated French chef takes nosh-ing to new heights and calorie lows.

If you're hosting any parties, you can set out a new breed of vegetable-intensive party munchies: low in fat and calories, high in fiber and nutrients, still crunchy and fun. Famed chef Jacques Pépin has developed snacks with all of these virtues. The French-born, classically trained chef grew up on—and cooked with—the cream, butter and other rich ingredients of his native cuisine. But times change, and he relocated. "It's not that all of a sudden I woke up and started cooking differently," he explains. "It has been a slow process that has evolved during my 30 years in the United States. It takes into account not only health concerns but also the new foods that are available here." Indeed, many of his new recipes are inspired by an international repertoire of "exotic" ingredients that would make a traditional French chef blanch: wonton wrappers, cannellini beans, jalapeño peppers and bulgur, to name a few. Once hard to find, these foods are becoming standard fare in many supermarkets.

Fresh herbs are also relative newcomers to many

supermarkets, and Pépin takes advantage of them for his lighter style of cooking. Fresh basil, dill, cilantro and other herbs figure prominently. So do calorie-free seasonings. "I use more garlic, vinegar, Tabasco and other ingredients that have a lot of flavor but little or no fat," Pépin explains. "I haven't eliminated anything; I just use more of the healthful ingredients."

But what to dip? The standard stuff is either boring or outrageously high in fat. Pépin suggests that you look to the vegetable section of your supermarket for fresh ideas. Any leaf or stick that's stiff enough to hold up a glob of dip can do the job.

*A **dazzling pepper platter.*** Slice and arrange raw orange, red, yellow, purple and green peppers.

Jícama. Peel and cut into sticks or rounds. This root vegetable has a sweet, crunchy taste, like an apple.

Celery root. Also called celeriac. A pungent relative of celery; peel and cut into sticks. (To prevent browning, dip in water with a little lemon juice.)

Baby veggies. Whole baby yellow and green squash, corn and carrots are much sweeter than the adult kinds.

Endive leaves. Each makes a little scoop, with a slightly bitter flavor.

Fennel bulb. Peel and cut into sticks. It offers a surprising licorice flavor.

EGG WHITES STUFFED WITH BULGUR

Per serving: 101 calories, 0.4 g. fat (4% of calories), 4.6 g. dietary fiber, 7.9 g. protein, 18 g. carbohydrates, 0 mg. cholesterol, 96 mg. sodium. Also a very good source of vitamin C.

Serves 6

⅔ **cup bulgur**
½ **cup finely chopped fresh parsley**
2 **scallions, trimmed and finely chopped**
2 **tablespoons lemon juice**
2 **tablespoons raisins**
1 **tablespoon finely chopped fresh mint**
1–2 **cloves garlic, finely chopped (1 teaspoon)**
1 **teaspoon finely chopped lemon rind**
½ **teaspoon seeded and chopped jalapeño peppers**
¼ **teaspoon hot-pepper sauce**
1 **small tomato**
9 **eggs**

1. Place the bulgur in a large bowl and cover with 3 cups water. Let stand for 1 hour. Drain well. Return the bulgur to the bowl and add the parsley, scallions, lemon juice, raisins, mint, garlic, lemon rind, peppers and hot-pepper sauce.

2. With a vegetable peeler, peel the tomato, reserving the peel. Seed the tomato and dice the flesh; add the tomatoes to the bulgur mixture. Mix well.

3. Bring another 3 cups water to a boil in a medium saucepan. Gently lower the eggs into the water and allow the water to return to a boil. Reduce the heat to low and gently cook the eggs for 9 minutes. Drain the water from the pan and shake the pan to crack the shells of the eggs. Fill the pan with ice and let the eggs cool completely in the ice.

4. Peel the eggs and halve lengthwise. Remove and discard the yolks. Fill each half with approximately 4 teaspoons of the bulgur mixture. Garnish with julienne strips of the reserved tomato peel.

EGGPLANT ORIENTAL ON TOMATO ROUNDS

Per serving: 45 calories, 1.1 g. fat (22% of calories), 2.3 g. dietary fiber, 1.5 g. protein, 8.7 g. carbohydrates, 0 mg. cholesterol, 352 mg. sodium.

Serves 6

2	eggplants (about 2 pounds total)
3½	tablespoons peeled and finely chopped fresh ginger
3	tablespoons chopped fresh cilantro
2	tablespoons soy sauce
5–6	cloves garlic, finely chopped
1	tablespoon rice-wine vinegar
1	teaspoon dark sesame oil
½	teaspoon granulated fructose
¼	teaspoon hot-pepper sauce
2	medium tomatoes, cut crosswise into 6 slices

1. Place the whole eggplants on a baking sheet and bake for 1 hour. Set aside to cool. When cool enough to handle, peel and dice.

2. Mix the ginger, cilantro, soy sauce, garlic, vinegar, oil, fructose and hot-pepper sauce in a large bowl. Add the eggplants and mix well. Arrange 2 tomato slices on each of 6 plates. Divide the eggplant mixture evenly on top of the tomato slices.

MICROWAVE POTATO CHIPS WITH SALSA CRUDA

Per serving: 152 calories, 0.4 g. fat (2% of calories), 4.1 g. dietary fiber, 5 g. protein, 35 g. carbohydrates, 0 mg. cholesterol, 19 mg. sodium. Also a very good source of vitamin C and potassium.

Serves 6

CHIPS

    3 large potatoes, peeled

SALSA

    2 medium tomatoes, peeled, seeded and chopped
    1 cup loosely packed chopped fresh cilantro
    1 medium onion, chopped
    1 small cucumber, trimmed, peeled, seeded and chopped
    4 scallions, finely chopped
    ¼ cup red-wine vinegar
  5–6 cloves garlic, finely chopped
    1 tablespoon seeded and finely chopped jalapeño peppers (wear plastic gloves when handling)
    ¼ teaspoon freshly ground black pepper

1. *To make the chips:* With a slicer, cut the potatoes into ¹⁄₁₆″ slices. Wash the slices in cool water and dry thoroughly. Arrange some of the slices on a waffled microwave tray and microwave on high for 5 minutes, or until crisp. Repeat with the remaining slices. Set aside.

2. *To make the salsa:* In a medium bowl, mix the tomatoes, cilantro, onions, cucumbers, scallions, vinegar, garlic, jalapeño peppers and black pepper. (For a smooth salad dressing, process the ingredients in blender.)

CREAMY CARAMELIZED GARLIC DIP

Per serving (2 tablespoons): 92 calories, 2.5 g. fat (24% of calories), 0.7 g. dietary fiber, 3.6 g. protein, 14.5 g. carbohydrates, 0 mg. cholesterol, 118 mg. sodium.

Makes 2½ cups

  1 **teaspoon + 2½ tablespoons canola oil**
  2 **heads garlic, halved crosswise**
  3 **tablespoons cider vinegar**
  2 **tablespoons chopped fresh tarragon**
  ¼ **teaspoon freshly ground black pepper**
  2 **cups nonfat plain yogurt**

1. Coat one side of an 8″ × 10″ piece of aluminum foil with 1 teaspoon oil. Arrange the garlic heads side by side on the foil, cut sides down, and wrap the foil around to encase the garlic. Place the foil package on a baking sheet and bake for 40 minutes. Set aside for 10 minutes to slightly cool.

2. Open the foil and press the cooked garlic flesh into the bowl of a food processor. Add the vinegar, tarragon and pepper. Process for 4 or 5 seconds, stopping once during processing to scrape the sides of the bowl.

3. Add the yogurt and process for about 30 more seconds, or until creamy. Add the remaining 2½ tablespoons oil and process until blended, about 15 seconds. Refrigerate, tightly covered, for up to 1 week. Serve with toasted rounds or a variety of crudités: carrot sticks, celery, broccoli and cauliflower florets.

Variation: The baked garlic can also be served on its own or as a garnish for roasted poultry.

Crunchy Bread Snacks

What do garlic bread and tortilla chips have in common? They're usually loaded with fat. Whip up your own ultra-low-fat, high-fiber versions to serve at parties.

Crispy garlic toast rounds. Slice French bread into ¼- to ½-inch-thick rounds. Spray a baking sheet with olive oil–based cooking spray. Lay the rounds on the baking sheet; brush lightly with olive oil or spray with cooking spray. Bake at 350° until brown, about 15 minutes. Remove and rub the rounds with a cut clove of garlic. Delicious with salsa!

Tortilla chips. Lightly brush a stack of flour tortillas with olive oil or spray with olive oil–based cooking spray. Cut each tortilla into eight wedges. Spray a baking sheet as above, then lay the tortilla wedges in alternate directions (to get the most on the baking sheet). Bake at 350° until golden, about six to eight minutes. Don't let them burn.

Nonfat pita chips. Separate pita pockets into two rounds. Lightly beat two egg whites and brush on the smooth outer side of each pocket. Cut each pita round into eight wedges. Bake at 350°, checking often, for ten minutes, or until crispy.

CANNELLINI BEAN HUMMUS

Per serving (2 tablespoons): 37 calories, 0.9 g. fat (22% of calories), 0.2 g. dietary fiber, 1.9 g. protein, 5.7 g. carbohydrates, 0 mg. cholesterol, 4 mg. sodium.

Makes 2¼ cups

 1 **cup fresh basil**
 1 **cup fresh parsley**
 4 **cloves garlic**
 ¼ **teaspoon freshly ground black pepper**
 1 **19-ounce can cannellini beans, drained**
 1 **tablespoon extra-virgin olive oil**
   Hot-pepper sauce

1. Bring 5 cups water to a boil in a large saucepan. Add the basil and parsley, pushing the herbs under the water. Cook for 10 seconds.

2. Drain the herbs in a colander, lightly pressing them to extract excess moisture. In a food processor, process the herbs with the garlic and pepper for a few seconds to combine, then scrape the sides of the bowl to gather the ingredients at the bottom.

3. Add the beans and process for 1 minute, stopping once or twice to scrape the sides of the bowl with a rubber spatula. The mixture should be smooth with green flecks. Add the oil and hot-pepper sauce to taste. Process for 5 more seconds. Transfer to a serving bowl and serve with dipping accompaniments.

PARMESAN WONTON CRISPS

Per serving: 79 calories, 0.6 g. fat (7% of calories), 1.3 g. carbohydrates, 2 mg. cholesterol, 185 mg. sodium.

Serves 6

18 wonton wrappers (3″ x 3″)
2 tablespoons grated Parmesan cheese

1. Bring about 2 quarts water to boil in a large pot. Add 9 wonton wrappers, dropping them into the water one at a time. Cook for 1½ minutes, then carefully remove with a skimmer and transfer to a large bowl of cold water.

2. Coat a 16″ × 14″ baking sheet with no-stick cooking spray. Carefully unfold the wrappers one at a time under water. Transfer them, still wet, to the baking sheet, arranging them side by side. Spray each wrapper with no-stick cooking spray. Sprinkle with 1 tablespoon Parmesan. Bake for 16 to 18 minutes. Repeat the procedure with the remaining 9 wrappers and 1 tablespoon Parmesan.

Variation: Sprinkle each batch of 9 wrappers with 1 teaspoon herbes de provence, a mixture of herbs commonly found in the south of France. Look for this mixture in the spice section of most well-stocked supermarkets.

—Cathy Perlmutter with Teresa Yeykal and Barb Fritz

Sunshine State Breakfasts

This fusion of Caribbean cuisines cooks up a spicy rainbow of waistline-friendly fare.

The first tentative rays of sunlight peek through louvered windows; outside, flamboyant green trees meld into sea grape bushes, soft, golden sand and turquoise sea. It's breakfast time in southern Florida. From Key West to Coral Gables, Coconut Grove to Little Havana, breakfast trays, buffet tables and kitchen counters are piled high with the bounty of the tropics.

Influenced by the cuisines of the Caribbean region and Central and South America, the southern Florida–Caribbean area has created a fusion cuisine all its own. Bustling kitchens, busy restaurants and sun-drenched markets are brimming with colorful fruits and vegetables, fresh seafood and lots of spices. These ingredients and ethnic cooking influences add up to a cuisine coined Floribbean, an exotic array of healthful, exciting food combinations.

The undisputed stars of the morning are tropical fruits—bananas, papayas, pineapples, guavas, mangoes. Floribbean cooks have learned to use these local fruits in innovative ways on breakfast tables: in juices and syrups, in pancakes and spreads, as nibbles and garnishes, even as ingredients for a Jamaican-inspired omelet.

The tastes are as vibrant as the backbeat of reggae music and as subtle as the soft slide of a merengue. Each bite of one of our Floribbean breakfasts brings a little tropical warmth into our lives.

Breakfast in a Glass

Some mornings are just too hectic for preparing breakfast. That's according to the mind. The body still needs nutrition. On those days, get a lift with a tropical breakfast in a glass. For the basic concoction, toss the following in a blender:

- 1 banana (frozen is best)
- ½ cup skim milk or nonfat yogurt
- 1 tablespoon oats (for fiber and thickness)

Then add a cornucopia of tropical-fruit combinations to your heart's content.

- ½ papaya, ½ cup grapefruit juice, a dash of nutmeg and a dash of allspice
- 1 mango, 1 teaspoon freshly grated ginger and the juice of 1 lime
- 1 cup pineapple juice (or 1½ cups pineapple chunks), 1 cup guava nectar, the juice of ½ lime and crushed mint leaves

VIBRANT EGG-WHITE OMELET

Per serving: 44 calories, 0 g. fat (0% of calories), 0.6 g. dietary fiber, 7.4 g. protein, 3.1 g. carbohydrates, 0 mg. cholesterol, 129 mg. sodium. Also a very good source of vitamin A, riboflavin and vitamin C.

Serves 4

- 1 **small yellow bell pepper, thinly julienned (½ cup)**
- 1 **small red bell pepper, thinly julienned (½ cup)**
- 1 **small green bell pepper, thinly julienned (½ cup)**
- 4 **sprigs fresh thyme, stripped and minced**
- ½ **teaspoon minced garlic**
- ½ **teaspoon minced canned jalepeño peppers**
  Freshly ground black pepper
- 8 **egg whites**
- 2 **tablespoons ice water**
  Sprigs of fresh thyme

1. Lightly coat a heavy, medium-size no-stick frying pan with cooking spray and place over medium heat. Add the yellow peppers, red peppers, green peppers and thyme and the garlic, jalepeño peppers and black pepper to taste. Sauté for 3 to 4 minutes, or until the vegetables are cooked. Reserve 1 tablespoon vegetables to sprinkle over the top as a colorful garnish.

2. Place the egg whites in a medium-size bowl. Add the ice water and whisk with a fork or wire whisk. Lightly coat a second medium-size no-stick frying pan or omelet pan with cooking spray and heat over medium heat.

3. When the pan is hot, add the egg whites and prepare as for any omelet. When the egg whites are cooked to the desired doneness, add the vegetable mixture, fold over and slide the omelet onto a heated plate.

4. Serve hot, garnished with the reserved vegetables and the thyme. Add a tropical-fruit parfait for a flavorful contrast.

BANANA PANCAKES

Per serving: 310 calories, 8.6 g. fat (25% of calories), 6.4 g. dietary fiber, 10.1 g. protein, 52.6 g. carbohydrates, 2.5 mg. cholesterol, 226 mg. sodium. Also a very good source of thiamin, riboflavin, niacin, vitamin B₆, folate, potassium and magnesium.

Serves 4

- 1⅓ **cups whole-wheat flour**
- 2 **teaspoons baking powder**
- 3 **ripe bananas, peeled**
- 2 **egg whites**
- 2 **tablespoons vegetable oil**
- 1 **cup 1% low-fat milk**

1. Sift the flour and baking powder into a small mixing bowl.

2. In a second, medium-size bowl, mash the bananas with a potato masher or the back of a fork until a thick paste has formed. Add the egg whites, oil and milk. Mix well. Slowly add the flour mixture, stirring until the batter has thickened.

3. Lightly coat a no-stick frying pan with cooking spray and place over medium heat. Slowly pour the batter into the pan to form 4″ pancakes. Cook, turning once, for 5 minutes, or until the pancakes are nicely browned on both sides. Repeat until all of the batter is used.

4. Serve hot with maple syrup, fruity preserves or a grinding of fresh nutmeg.

CORNMEAL PORRIDGE

Per serving: 202 calories, 1.9 g. fat (8% of calories), 8.2 g. dietary fiber, 4.16 g. protein, 44 g. carbohydrates, 0 mg. cholesterol, 26 mg. sodium. Also a very good source of vitamin C and magnesium.

Serves 4

PORRIDGE

    1½ **cups yellow cornmeal**

SAUCE

    2 **medium carambolas**
    ½ **cup cubed fresh mangoes**
    ½ **teaspoon blackstrap molasses**
      Sliced carambolas
      Sprigs of fresh mint

1. *To make the porridge:* Heat 4 cups water to boiling in a medium-size saucepan. Slowly pour in the cornmeal, stirring constantly with a wire whisk. Cook over low heat for 4 to 5 minutes, or until the porridge is cooked to your taste. (It's important to keep stirring to avoid lumps.)

2. *To make the sauce:* Place the whole carambolas and mangoes into the bowl of a food processor. Pulse until you have a thick paste. Spoon the paste into a small serving bowl and swirl the molasses through it with a fork.

3. Spoon the porridge into soup bowls and garnish with the carambola slices and mint. Serve with a splash of low-fat milk and sweeten with a drizzle of the carambola-mango sauce.

—Jessica B. Harris with Mary Nagle, Barb Fritz, Teresa Yeykal and the Rodale Test Kitchen

Credits

"The C Factor" on page 71 is adapted from "The C Factor" by Robert Sweetgall, which originally appeared in *Walking* magazine. Copyright © 1994 by Robert Sweetgall. Reprinted by permission. Robert Sweetgall is the author of *Walking Off Weight* and *Walk the Four Seasons: Walking and Cross-Training Logbook*. For more information, call 1-800-762-9255.

"Fat or Fiction?" on page 78 is adapted from "Fat or Fiction?" by Jayne Hurley, which originally appeared in *Nutrition Action Healthletter*. Copyright © 1994, Center for Science in the Public Interest.

"Hidden Sugar Revealed" on page 85 is adapted from "Hidden Sugar" by Michele Meyer, which originally appeared in *SELF* magazine. Copyright © 1995 by Michele Meyer. Reprinted with permission.

"What's in a Label?" on page 91 is adapted from "What's in a Label?" by Bonnie Liebman, which originally appeared in *Nutrition Action Healthletter*. Copyright © 1994, Center for Science in the Public Interest.

"More Fat Than Meets the Eye" on page 94 is adapted from "Behind the News" in *Nutrition Action Healthletter*. Copyright © 1994, Center for Science in the Public Interest.

"The Brave New World of Food Science" on page 98 is adapted from "1995 Nutrition Report" by William Grimes, which originally appeared in *SELF* magazine. Copyright © 1995 by William Grimes. Reprinted by permission.

"The Commonsense, All-You-Need Diet" on page 100 is adapted from "Commonsense All-You-Need Diet" by Corby Kummer, which originally appeared in *SELF* magazine. Copyright © 1995 by Corby Kummer. Reprinted by permission.

277

Index